PRAISE FOR JAY GLAZER AND
UNBREAKABLE

"Jay Glazer has lived *Unbreakable* his entire life. More importantly, behind the grit and toughness is a compassionate and warm human being. Everyone who's had a chance to get to know him would repeat the same stories of trust, reliability, and loyalty. It's simply how he is wired, and I'm quite sure you'll feel that in *Unbreakable*."

—Sean Payton,
head coach of the New Orleans Saints

"*Unbreakable* is more than just a book title; Unbreakable is more than just the name of his gym; as someone who's known him for nearly thirty years, I can tell you that UNBREAKABLE is what Jay is as a person. I've seen it; it hasn't always been pretty, but it's always been open and honest. The beauty now is that he's sharing this honesty with the world to remind us that we're not alone in whatever our personal struggles may be. This book chronicles a life of not only overturning obstacles but turning them into building blocks. Like Jay, it's real, raw, life-affirming, and a laugh riot. No, that's not a typo; even though he tackles the hard stuff, you're guaranteed to laugh the entire time."

—Curt Menefee,
cohost of *FOX NFL Sunday*

"Jay is real, and that is what makes him great. But what's consistent about Jay is his loyalty. You can ALWAYS count on him. *Unbreakable* reminds me of this: Jay's can-do and will-do attitude. In a world of 'what have you done for me lately' or 'what can you do for me now,' Jay stands out as a real one."

—Chuck Liddell,
former UFC light heavyweight champion,
UFC Hall of Famer

"As a woman, veteran, and athlete, forged by tough love, I initially under-estimated just how much Jay's friendship, mentorship, and insights into mental toughness and vulnerability would shape my life. *Unbreakable* en-courages readers to unlock their potential, lean into the uncomfortable, and stand proud of what makes them different."

—Kirstie Ennis, U.S. Marine Corps sergeant and door gunner,
Paralympic snowboarding athlete, first female above-the-knee amputee
to summit Mount Kilimanjaro

"Get ready for a fireside chat! I have never read a book so authentic to a writer's true personality. This read is as close as you get to having a one-on-one drink or dinner with Jay. Not only is he unapologetically honest about his struggle, but he also shows us how we can collectively overcome and make progress, through one another, like he has. Jay's *Unbreakable* lays down a road map to strengthen yourself mentally and physically in every journey ahead of you. Be ready to laugh your ass off, cry like the vulnerable warriors we all are, and be inspired!"

—Josh Burris, CEO of GNC

"Jay's a fighter, in every sense of the word. He's not only Unbreakable; he's an underdog who believes in people so much that it helps them believe in themselves. I am one of those people."

—Nate Boyer, Green Beret, Bronze Star recipient, former Seattle Seahawk

"Jay Glazer helps people look forward and know that it's okay to be dif-ferent, because we all are. *Unbreakable* is inspiring and motivational. It teaches people that the phrase 'I got your back' is for always, and that you are never alone."

—Royce Gracie, first-ever UFC champion,
UFC Hall of Famer, and Gracie Jiu-Jitsu practitioner

"I attended MVP for the first time several years ago. I had hit rock bot-tom when I attempted suicide twice in three months. When I finally real-ized I wasn't happy with myself, I started doing the work to get back to being the version of myself I was happy with.

"Being in MVP with Jay made me proud. I stopped trying to be like other people and started celebrating what makes me great. Today, I stand taller when I walk into rooms. I think my voice matters, and I take up space. I am willing to push myself because I know that I have a team of amazing people who always have my back. Reading *Unbreakable* is just like becoming part of Jay's team."

—Danielle Baker, U.S. Army 10th Mountain Division, chemical operations specialist, one hundred percent disabled combat veteran

"Jay has always had an unmatched passion and desire to help others, but as Jay's friend and business partner, what has been so amazing is witnessing his personal growth. In *Unbreakable*, his ability to help others has been elevated to a whole new level."

—Lindsey Berg, two-time captain of the U.S. Women's Olympic Volleyball team, and two-time silver medalist

"This book is one of the most meaningful books I've ever read. It's raw and real, coupled with compelling writing and entertaining moments. Like Jay Glazer, *Unbreakable* is also one of a kind. Read it and become Unbreakable!"

—Jon Gordon, twelve-time bestselling author of twenty-four books, including *The Energy Bus*

"Jay Glazer sits at the intersection of authenticity and heart in everything he does. Jay has impacted many lives with his genuine vulnerability and grit, creating a space of belonging for those around him. *Unbreakable* is no different, offering an impassioned invitation to be and to own your own unique self with everything you do."

—Kami Craig, two-time Olympic gold medalist in water polo

"From the day I met Jay Glazer, I recognized his ability to turn scars into superpowers. He is an inspiring example of a kind character who sets an example of wearing one's adversities like badges of honor and embracing one's vulnerability as a signature of human courage. *Unbreakable* proves this fantastically."

—Hayley Paige, famed wedding gown designer

UN BREAK ABLE

HOW I TURNED MY DEPRESSION AND ANXIETY INTO MOTIVATION AND YOU CAN TOO

JAY GLAZER

WITH **SARAH TOMLINSON**

DEY ST.
An Imprint of WILLIAM MORROW

DEY ST.

This book attempts to present a different perspective on depression, and advocate for people suffering to reach out to others for support. This book is written as a source of information only. The information contained in this book should by no means be considered a substitute for the advice, decisions or judgment of the reader's physician or other professional advisor.

The author and the publisher expressly disclaim responsibility for any adverse effects arising from the use or application of the information contained herein.

FIRST EDITION

Library of Congress Cataloging-in-Publication Data has been applied for.

ISBN 978-0-06-306285-6

33614082768226

22 23 24 25   LSC   10 9 8 7 6 5 4 3 2

To everybody who's different, everybody who's been through the shit, everybody who's gone through that tunnel and come out on the other side, everybody who's fought back against the gray, and everybody who wants to make the world the way it's supposed to be—one united world under God, with all our differences put aside, so we can be of service to one another

CONTENTS

FOREWORD BY
DWAYNE "THE ROCK" JOHNSON

Jay Glazer is an amazing human being.

I've gotten close with him over the course of almost fifteen years of knowing each other, and I can tell you with no absence of clarity that he's "one of one."

NOT BECAUSE OF all his success and fame, but because of all his failures and scars.

You see, Jay wears failure like a badge of courage.

And the scars he proudly wears—both physical and emotional. They all tell the story of a powerful and higher calling.

OVER THE YEARS, I've come to realize there's a reason why Jay is highly respected and loved in every circle he walks into . . . it's because he lives for his TEAM. He lives to LAUGH and most importantly, Jay Glazer LIVES TO BE OF SERVICE.

THOSE ARE THE three critical pillars Jay lives by daily, which he shares in this book.

But there's one more thing that makes Jay a helluva human being.

IT'S NOT SOMETHING he LIVES FOR, but rather a place he understands deeply what it's like to LIVE IN.

THAT PLACE IS simply called the gray.

The mental health stuff.

That hard stuff.

The stuff a lot of people don't like to talk about, especially us men.

That's the gray that Jay embraces and talks about with openness and vulnerability.

The gray that Jay helps to empower other people through that ultimately helps change their lives.

WE ALL HAVE our scars, and we all have our experiences in the gray, and in Jay we all have someone to lean on when the mental going gets tough.

AND THAT'S WHY my friend is so rare and one amazing human being.

PROUD OF YOU, brother. Cheers to always finding "color" in our gray.

LOVE YOU, BRO, and congrats again!

Dwayne "The Rock" Johnson

INTRODUCTION

Going from Broke to Unbreakable

A re you KIDDING ME?! I can't go to the bathroom because
the refrigerator blocks your bathroom door?!" Michael
Strahan screeched at me, in my shitty fourth-floor walkup
on East 91st Street in New York City, light years before he was
the king of daytime television.

"You can go to the bathroom, you just can't shut the door.
Make do," I yelled back, total problem solver that I am.

"What the f— . . . " His voice trailed off. "Jay, the light
doesn't work in here, I can't see shit!"

"Stray, just hold down the string attached to the light bulb.
Keep it pulled down the whole time and the light will stay on."
Stray is the nickname those who are close to him use, though
on this day I was about to call him one of the *many* other nick-
names I've had for him over the years.

"What if I have to sit down?" he asked.

I thought for a second. "I haven't figured that part out yet.
Just keep the door open so the light comes in. Trust me, I won't
watch."

"Jay, you gotta be . . . I don't even know what to say."

"Hey Stray, one of us ain't a six-five, 272-pound pass rusher, getting paid millions of bucks to play for the Giants, so just fucking make do. This is what nine grand a year gets me!"

It was 9,450 bucks a year to be precise. And this tiny shoebox, six blocks from Spanish Harlem, was all I could afford for the decade I was hustling, slowly but relentlessly, toward my dreams. I was so broke that Mr. "I'm Too Good to Go to the Bathroom and Hold the String" volunteered to drive me from Giants Stadium, where I was cutting my teeth on being an NFL reporter, back to New York City every single night, for SIX years! Basically, I owe him about twenty-eight grand in Lincoln Tunnel fare.

Our friendship had been forged instantly in '93, our first year at Giants training camp, when nobody paid any attention to us. Well, let me correct that. They talked to him, but it was to make sure he paid for all the veteran players' dinners and sometimes their big bar tabs, an old hazing ritual for young players. That's a good twenty-five to thirty big, big eaters. *Welcome to the NFL, Michael.* Trust me, funding nights out for wild players like Lawrence Taylor was not exactly a fun way for Stray to spend his money.

As for me? The other reporters openly made fun of my brotherly relationship with Michael. So, I was broke *and* the brunt of everyone's jokes. But fuck them. If I wasn't going to be on their team, I would start my own. Yup, a team for a whopping two of us!

Michael and I shared a juvenile sense of humor, and we both worked ten million times harder than anyone else in the room. So, even though his hard work would pay off way before mine did, and he would become the Giants' star pass rusher, our brotherhood grew because of our shared work ethic. I think he respected that I jostled for every possible freelance gig, on top of having a weekly one-hour show for NY1 TV and a weekly column in the *New York Post*, just to scrape up my $910 a month for rent.

Hard work does pay off though. In the twenty-five years since my brother (or baby sister as I still refer to him, just to piss him off) couldn't shut the bathroom door in my apartment, I became one of the top inside sports reporters on the planet, as FOX Sports' NFL Insider. I've had the biggest scoops in NFL history, involving the most well-known names in football (including, perhaps, the biggest: the Spygate video that caught the New England Patriots cheating). I've covered twenty-five Super Bowls. Been a part of eight Super Bowl broadcasts. Got inducted into the Television Hall of Fame with Terry Bradshaw, Howie Long, Strahan, Jimmy Johnson, and Curt Menefee and the entire *FOX NFL Sunday* team. Created the first mixed martial arts cross-training program for pro athletes and trained over a thousand NFLers, fighters, and pro athletes. Became an actor (I use the term veryyyyy loosely) and a regular cast member on the highest-rated comedy on HBO, *Ballers*, with my little niece Dwayne "The Rock" Johnson, for five seasons. Opened Unbreakable Performance Center, which quickly became named "The Most Elite Gym in America" by Yahoo Health. And this is the most important one . . . became a voice for mental health—a mental health warrior, if you will—and saved the lives of countless combat veterans and retired athletes through my charity, MVP: Merging Vets & Players. I have coached people out of suicide and hopelessness every week and worked my ass off to beat down the negative stigma often associated with mental health issues. God has blessed me with the ability to communicate, to be authentic, and to relate to any and all. And in turn, I have made it my life's mission to lift up others.

Sounds like a dream life, right? I mean, I am still waiting to wake up in fifth grade and find out that none of this shit happened. What most of you don't know is that I accomplished all of this while living in my own painful, dark cell of depression and anxiety. Mental health is the hip, hot thing to talk about these days, and it's about damn time. But I have been privy to the painful reality of this issue for far too long.

Despite the laughs on TV and the crazy, riotous stories I am fond of telling, I have lived life in the gray since I was a kid. Life in the gray . . . this phrase has found its way into my daily vocabulary since I first heard it and felt like it exactly described how it feels to be me. I wake up every single morning, convinced the sky is falling; and it's this heavy sadness that exhausts me, drags me down, and eventually drowns me. Even with meds (the other four-letter word that has been prevalent in my life), and every other form of therapy I could try, the gray has clung to me.

In the last few years, I have found ways to crack through the gray and see . . . dare I say it . . . some slivers of blue. (I am afraid to say I found a way to the blue, because people with depression get scared to jinx it when we find something that actually works.) If you are reading this and are wondering what the blue feels like, because you haven't yet seen that sliver, I absolutely fucking get you, I understand you, I hurt for you, but most of all . . . I GOT YOUR BACK! And I hope that the tools in this book help you find a way there. In turn, I can also learn from you, as we all start talking publicly about our fears and anxieties more.

The world is my locker room, and my locker room is filled

with a wild blend of characters who fit together in my sense of crazy that adds up to a team. In the real world, you might never find a place where Sly Stallone; Kirstie Ennis, a female marine door gunner who lost her leg in a helicopter crash; Usher; Snoop Dogg; Wiz Khalifa; Demi Lovato; and Lindsey Berg, the captain of the US Olympic Volleyball Team would all be teammates. In my world? That's a normal Tuesday. In my world, all of these different people fit beautifully together and help each other in ways you would never expect. And now, by reading this book, you're on our team too.

Being a part of a team that has my back, and which makes me constantly laugh, has been one of the best antidotes to my depression. There's nothing lonelier than pretending everything is fine. Honesty is the cost of admission to this team. And it's the secret weapon for healing, connecting, and fighting on the journey from the gray to the blue. That's because vulnerability is true strength. If I am vulnerable, it may inspire a teammate to be the same. It may help lift them out of their own pit.

This book is not your typical memoir. It is not your typical self-help book either. This is a journey that I'm taking with you—with all my readers, all of us together—to help us, where the gray has taken life over, to find the blue cracks. Throughout this journey, I hope to help you feel empowered by your scars and fuckedupness. It's okay to be fucked up, truly. I'm fucked up, but the difference now is that I'm good with my fuckedupness. And my fuckedupness empowers me; it doesn't make me damaged. If you've ever felt the universe is against you, if you can't ever "catch a break," if you feel the constant uphill-in-wet-cement climb that is depression . . . I understand you, I relate to you, I am you.

As you read this book, I will tell you the stories of how I

came to accept my fuckedupness, came to help others accept theirs, and found ways to work with it and even against it. The details of my methods are specific to me and my life; to you, they may sound extreme, crazy, or totally out of reach. Your life is not my life. Remember two things as you read these stories: First, I'm telling you my stories to entertain you (they are pretty nuts). Second, my stories are meant as examples, illustrations of what I'm trying to teach you. So, when I talk about telling Demi Lovato to never be late to practice for our fight team (wow, this sentence seems ridiculous, even to me), don't think "Well, good for you man, I don't know Demi Lovato." Instead, come up with *your* version of a way to find and build your team, however that is possible in your world. You get me?

So why listen to me? These are life lessons I've learned, via real experiences: what can work and how to keep at it, even on the days that go from gray to black to bleak, no matter how hard you try to talk, joke, or fight your way out of the morass. Whether you're looking down the barrel of the gray yourself, struggling against its weight, or you're just wanting to get better, and to be better to others in your life, to build your business and improve your relationships, this is a guidebook that can help you.

I'll bring you inside the locker rooms of the world's most successful athletes and coaches, on set with your favorite TV stars, and inside the gyms where veterans physically and mentally get their fight back, and I'll teach you what I've learned from all of them.

At the same time, we're going to talk about the hardest stuff there is in these pages—depression, anxiety, the shittiness of the gray, and the carnage they often cause. But we are also going to laugh our asses off along the way. Holy shnikees, will we laugh, because humor is one of the most powerful medicines that helps combat the gray.

We've got our work cut out for us. The world is scarier now than perhaps ever before. Social media makes us feel left out and often bullied. We constantly see online hate, and pressure is at an all-time high. We just fought through a pandemic—a war none of us signed up for.

WE together can bond over our fuckedupness. WE together can lift each other up in our journeys. WE together can empower others. I don't know if we are going to save the world, but we are damn sure going to improve it, as my MVP teammate, and beautiful badass Marine door gunner and now amputee and Purple Heart recipient, Kirstie Ennis said.

So, now is the time to lift each other in order to embrace our scars, embrace our fuckedupness, but also to bring hope to the darkness, to help all of you, because YOU DESERVE IT!

Allow me to lift you up, teammate, so that you can lift me up as well.

I need it.

OUTWORK THE WORLD
AND BE THE LAST
ONE STANDING

The two questions I get asked the most in my life (Besides "Hey Jay, I have this great business idea for The Rock, can you give me his number?" Dead serious.) are: "How the fuck did you get here?" and "Why does everybody trust you enough to give you inside information?"

My journey began on a stage at Boston Comedy Club in the Greenwich Village neighborhood of NYC. Four years before I would ever step foot in an NFL locker room, nearly twenty years before I broke Spygate and Congress called looking for my copy of the tape, threatening jail time if I told them to fuck off (which I did). Nearly thirty years before I would actually get to use my comedy chops on screen when I got thrown into *Ballers* on HBO, or rather when I strong-armed myself onto that show (trust me, more on that later). Yup, this journey starts not in sports but in my quest to make people laugh.

"Ladies and gentlemen, all the way from his high school wrestling days, here to the stage at Boston Comedy Club, the one, the only, JAY GLAZER," famed comedian Jay Mohr announced to a somewhat packed crowd, introducing me for my first ever stand-up comedy show.

My routine? The same wise-ass sarcasm that I use to this day. One of my bits was me explaining that world problems should be settled the old-fashioned way, and thus I nominated Mike Tyson as the president of the United States. I then began to imitate Iron Mike in all sorts of political situations, which usually ended with Mike taking a world leader behind a 7-Eleven and kicking the shit out of him. I think I was ahead of my time as a political think tanker.

This was my first ever stab at standup, and yet I won the Open Mic Night contest that evening. But even greater than the win was the high that comedians often live off of, the type that spikes their adrenaline. Let's just say I needed that boost even more than most people. We'll get into why later in these pages.

Little did I know as I walked off that stage that the wheels would be put in motion at that very moment to change my life forever . . . all it would take was one chance meeting, or as I like to think of it, the universe conspiring *for* me, and my career in sports would begin! After my set, I was immediately approached by a really nice man (trust me, I don't often assign this designation) named David Blatt.

"You were really funny," he said. "That was your first time? Wow, that's pretty ballsy."

One thing I don't lack are balls. Wait, I totally could have written that better but, fuck it, let me keep my ADD on track.

"I understand you want to get into sports," he continued. "I'm a producer at CBS Sports. I can get you a job there with us."

Really? Holy shit, a job at CBS Sports? Wow, I'm still in

college, and here I am hitting the big time already? What are we talking about here? Hosting? Producing? Sideline reporter? NFL analyst? Sports was everything to me. I'd always been an unhappy, scared little kid, and sports was my escape. It offered inclusion for everyone, even guys like me who were small and weren't ever going to play in the NFL. We could be general managers, scouts, reporters—hell, anyone could be a fan. Instant team! Friends, I had a Dallas Cowboy–themed bar mitzvah. I'd always known I was going to be in the sports world somehow, and now it was happening. Even if it wasn't going to happen quite like I'd imagined it—at least not right away.

"I can probably get you in logging tape," David said flatly. "It's fifty bucks a day, and you'll pretty much be locked in a room down in the catacombs of CBS, away from everyone else. You'll be assigned a game, or a tennis or golf tournament, and you'll log down on a paper every single thing that happens, on every play or swing, whatever that is," he said, deflating my delusions of grandeur and immediate stardom. "I know it's only fifty bucks, but are you good with that?"

Hey, it was a start. Oh, and that name, David Blatt, remember that name. The journey to success is about building a team, walking the walk with as many people as you can.

Well, that tape logging gig, plus my stand-up comedy experience got me an unpaid internship at Sportsradio 66 WFAN in New York, the first all-sports radio station in America. THIS was the big time, even though it was, well, fifty bucks a day less than CBS paid me, for a whopping ZERO dollars! But to me, experience and connections were more valuable than dollars, though the dollars would have certainly allowed me to live a much safer existence.

This was at the height of WFAN's initial popularity. Some

of its hosts like Mike and The Mad Dog and Imus in the Morning were rock stars. And even though I wasn't getting paid, I was part of it. My job duties at WFAN? Welp, they consisted of oh-so-glamorous tasks like taking Mike Francesca to and from the bathroom at The NFL Draft, so nobody would bother him. Or fetching coffee and ordering dinners for the overnight host and producer. But I eventually graduated up to the coveted position of answering and screening calls from fans who were trying to get on the show. I affectionately referred to my position as Pissboy, or rather Associate Pissboy, but hey, even pissboys gotta start somewhere.

But one thing I intentionally did when I interned there—and this is a lesson for all aspiring whatevers, in whatever field you want to break into—**I did everything I could to *stand out!* Don't just quietly go about your business. Stand the fuck out!** (Side note: now that I own my own business, I can wholeheartedly tell you, from the vantage point of an employer, that I absolutely love, love, love when someone stands outs and takes the initiative to show me that they can get things done. It's rarer than you may realize.) So, I volunteered to do things that generally didn't ever get covered at WFAN. I asked to go to press conferences and gather tape of interviews. I volunteered to go to the NFL Draft and do whatever pissboy job they had for me there (hence me and Francesca's shmekel taking multiple bathroom runs). Oh, I also had to literally run bases for Francesca when he was at bat on the WFAN Softball team. Hey, I got my own jersey and everything. Look, Mom, between me being a bodyguard for Francesca's dick and running bases for him, I made it, Mom, I made it!

The point is, I stood out. I asked the producers and hosts there every single week for tips of the craft, lessons about how they made it to their positions, if I could practice other jobs there that I wanted to learn. I offered to be free labor on anything and everything, and I was absolutely relentless and persistent about it. (You can persist, as long as it's done with a fun tone, so it doesn't become annoying and always . . . *always* show gratitude for someone's time.)

I had done enough thankless tasks to be one of the very few people to ever intern twice at The FAN (as it was affectionately known over the years). My simply being there for two semesters eventually led me to my first actual paid job, as associate editor, covering the New York Giants for a weekly thirty-six-page newsmagazine, based solely on the Giants. And I got paid . . . drumroll pleeeease . . . $24,000 per year. Jackpot! That was all gravy until my third week on the job when the paper went Chapter 11 and they stopped paying me. They still produced the publication, and despite me no longer getting actual money to write and edit it, they still published my stories, which became my way into the NFL journalism world.

Not only was this my in, but it is the foundation of a philosophy I would come to strictly live and die by to this day. My first day covering the Giants, July 25, 1993, I walked into the Giants locker room to report on the start of that year's NFL training camp and looked around, knowing I had everything against me. This was the mecca of media. I had no experience compared to the other reporters, TV personalities, radio voices, etc. I had no education compared to them. I had no know-how of the ins and outs of the job. So that day, since I couldn't compete on their terms, and I knew I had to survive somehow, I surveyed my options. I still don't know where these came from, whether it was God, or me tapping into the future coach I would become. But I took some advice my dad had once given me, about getting ahead by being loyal and outworking the world, and I spun it out into three mantras I would use to make me stand out:

I. Be different

II. Outwork the world

III. Be the last one standing

"HOW CAN I BE DIFFERENT?" Instead of trying to hide, or apologize for, the ways in which I wasn't like the other reporters, I vowed to take my differences and turn them into my secret weapons. In doing so, I would stand out, and my reporting and writing would too.

"OUTWORK THE WORLD." If the others worked nine to five, I would work from seven a.m. to seven p.m. I would outwork them all, not by a little, but by a lot! It's a trait that every successful person on the planet shares. It would go on to become a pillar of my Unbreakable Mindset, something I'll dive into in great detail later in this book.

"BE THE LAST ONE STANDING." Which meant I would never, EVER, ever give up.

So back to "being different." For starters, I decided I would approach this job *differently* than everyone else. For example, instead of focusing on the scoops, I would focus on the relationships. The scoops would come with those. I didn't have the words to express it this way at the time, but I've always needed teams. I've needed genuine bonds in my life, for my own stability and mental health—for my survival. And back then, I was so broke, it wasn't just my emotional survival that was on the line either. Sometimes I needed a ride. Sometimes I needed a free meal. Always, I needed to know people had my back. So, I built myself into the social structure of the locker room with those players. We laughed a ton together. I was very, very, very real with them when they were fucking up. And I was just as real with them about my own struggles. They asked me for advice on a million things regarding their off-the-field lives.

It's interesting. The first fifteen or so years of using this approach, I got absolutely murdered by many of the other reporters, decimated for having these friendships. They thought I was using the players and not being objective. I felt they weren't being objective by killing a player because he wouldn't talk to them. Which is worse? But what the reporters never fully grasped was, I wasn't building these relationships solely for scoops. I was building myself a team, a network who understood people like me and my fuckedupness. The players got it; the reporters really didn't.

Over time, I expanded those relationships and networks to include coaches, personal assistants, shit, even ball boys. Whoever I could get on my team was welcome. I judged no one so there were no exceptions. All the while, I would make sure I always pointed out to these same players/coaches/executives what made me different from the rest. I not only embraced my differences, I made my battle to excel in spite of them everyone else's fight as well. I was a relationship builder. To this day it's probably what I do best. I connect with people and then connect people to each other. But a side benefit is that from relationships comes the ever-valuable INFORMATION! Relationships are everything!

But no relationship would ever become as important to me, or as cherished, as the very first player I'd become friends with from Day One of Training Camp. He was orthodontically challenged and was drafted to replace Lawrence Taylor's sack production (while LT was still on the team). What a recipe for disaster for this poor bastard. We were in similar boats. Very few talked to either one of us—they made fun of us, actually.

Here I was, getting made fun of ferociously, by many of the other members of the media, as well as some members of the Giants' front office. But, man, there was something special about that dude, and he saw something special in me, so we just latched onto each other. I was there for him when they moved his position because he couldn't beat out these other two guys. I was there for him when they were calling him a bust. Similarly, he was there for me when I couldn't even pay my way to and from Giants Stadium. He was there when the other reporters laughed at my interview questions.

That player was Michael Strahan. He changed my life forever. Honestly, I don't know where I would be without the guy. He legitimized me to the other players, assuring them that I'd always be true to my most golden rule of all the golden rules . . . Trust.

"You can TRUST Jay!" Michael told anyone who would listen.

Trust.

That's the secret ingredient to being an NFL Insider. Gain trust. And never ever, ever fuck that trust over. (Also an important ingredient for being a good teammate, which we'll get to a little later.) It didn't take long for that trust to build to another level inside that Giants locker room. The more members of the Giants' brass told the players NOT to talk to me, the more some players would angrily say, "They are trying to TELL ME what I can and can't do? Fuck that, don't tell my ass what to do. So, here, Jay, here's our fucking game plan!"

Literally, guys would give me their game plans as a way to claim their own independence (alpha males do not like being told what they CAN'T do). Every week I would do the exact same thing with those game plans, which was . . . *absolutely nothing*. I knew they were giving them to me out of emotion. I didn't want them to regret it, and by sitting on them, I earned their trust even more. I never wanted players to be sorry they'd shared something or to hurt their chances of winning on Sundays. Those players recognized this, and it made them trust me even more.

A few months into covering the Giants, I got my big break . . . well, it's all relative, as you might've guessed by now. I got a show on NY1 TV, a one-hour, weekly, call-in program where I gave deep, deep insight into the Giants. Inside information you couldn't hear anywhere else. For the first few years my salary was, hold up, let me add this all up right . . . OK, carry the zero . . . OK, got it . . . my salary was a grand total of $0. But the experience was worth more than gold. Every single Friday night I went to 42nd and Tenth in New York City to do a midnight show. I know, not exactly a prime-time slot, but damn, I made it must-watch TV if you were a Giants fan. An hour of the most inside Giants news you could get, anywhere on the planet. Can you guess the very, very first guest I had come on with me? Yep, dressed sharply in his Coogi sweater, the incomparable Michael Strahan.

A year or two in, the guy who was covering the Jets at the time asked for a paycheck. They said no, so they asked if I could do the Jets too. I bullshitted my way in by proclaiming, albeit falsely, "Sure, I'm tied into the Jets' locker room too."

Only, I wasn't . . . at first. However, I had my friends on the Giants—like Strahan, Jumbo Elliott, Jessie Armstead, Percy Ellsworth, Brandon Short, William Roberts—call their friends on the Jets to get me all lined up. Suddenly, I graduated up to having a weekly Giants and Jets show every Friday night at NY1 TV for, yup, still a whopping zero dollars.

So, not only would I throw myself into outworking the competition at my reporting gig, I also had the full-time job of, well, needing to find a PAYING full-time job. I paid my own way to other cities, to just walk in and ask to meet with editors or producers and try to convince them I was worth taking a flyer on, because I would outwork every other motherfucker in the world. This literally went on for TEN years until I got my first full-time gig. Ten brutal years of rejections, ten brutal years of not knowing how I was ever going to pay my rent. Ten brutal years of being told I wasn't good enough. During that time, instead of trying to change myself to be more like whatever those editors and producers wanted, I asked myself, again and again:

"How can I be different?"

And I made good on my vow to outwork the world. But this is where I took it up a notch. I accepted yet another gig, for yup, you know the answer, zero bucks . . . this time a Monday Night Football Giants/Jets radio show on WABC Radio. I had a different player, or players, come into Mickey Mantle's restaurant in NYC and "co-host" with me for *three hours!* I sold them on coming in as a chance for them to work on their public speaking skills and, get this, a free dinner at Mickey Mantle's. Every player I asked came in for me. Every single one. They drove, traffic and all, into the city to sit there with my crazy, broke ass for three hours each Monday night. God Almighty, I've been blessed.

Free steak dinners aside, it wasn't all glorious. Because I was still so broke, I was trying my hand at newspaper, TV, and now radio journalism, hoping one would eventually lead to a full-time job, which I still badly needed.

I did that for years. Years and years of working on my craft, getting better in front of the camera, or on radio, and telling anyone and everyone who would listen that I had a show on WABC and NY1 TV. I worked every single week to improve, while basically wondering if anyone was watching. One night, I found out that, in fact, someone was.

He was Steve Serby, a longtime columnist for the *New York Post*. His belief in me changed my life, for which I will forever be appreciative.

Serby called the NY1 control room after a show, at about one a.m. "Jay, Steve Serby here at the *Post*. You have built more relationships than I've ever seen in such a short period. I think you should work at the *Post*! What do you think? How would you like a job at the *Post*?"

Ummmm, are you fucking kidding me? Where and when do I start, and how much do I get paid?

Once again, my big break appeared closer than it actually was. Serby brought me in to talk with the editor of the *Post*, the legendary Greg Gallo. Holy fuck was this guy straight out of a comic book. He was pretty much a dead ringer, at least in how he acted, for the editor from *Spider Man*—a trait that I consider a compliment—and we got a kick out of each other. Once again, I bullshitted my way in. I had zero real writing experience; only little crappy articles I'd written in that *Giants Extra* magazine. And this was the *Post*, one of the epicenters of sports reporting in *the* epicenter of sports.

"OK, we have this new phenom going to St. John's University named Felipe Lopez, who is supposed to be the next Michael Jordan," Gallo said to me in his office. "Serby says if I put you on this beat, you'll end up getting invited over to his house for dinner."

"Every Wednesday," I said, *way* too cocky for my own good.

"Well, I can't just give you college basketball, I need to see what you can do. Go to St. John's and get me a story on Lopez."

So, I took a few subways to a bus or two, on the $15 I had to my name at the time, to the campus of St. John's and just struck up conversation after conversation, until eventually, enough people led me to Felipe Lopez himself. I introduced myself and, just like I had done in the Giants locker room, I got him to understand my plight and struggle: "Hey man, if I can just get a few minutes of your time, I haven't had a full-time job, ever, in this business. This is a shot for me to actually get a full-time gig, and all I need from you is to give me five minutes. May not seem like a lot to you, or may seem like it's too much for you, but man, it would mean a ton to me."

Lesson here: don't act too cool for school. Allow others to have empathy for you. All those players in the Giants locker room, I let them know my struggle. I was vulnerable about it, brought them into my plight. Take your ego away and replace it with honesty and vulnerability. I believe that people are intrinsically good and have the natural capacity to empathize with others. Sometimes they just need you to open the door for them to do so, and to join your team.

"OK, you got it. I may not say much, but yeah, I will sit down with you," Lopez said.

BAM, there it was, my first ever, EVER, EVER exclusive for the *New York Post*, and it was only for a try-out article. Lopez didn't say anything exciting and kept his answers very short, a few words per sentence, but it was the first time he sat down to "talk" to any local reporter. The *Post* splashed it all over their back page. So, as I churn out these book pages with gratitude (living in gratitude is another powerful antidepressant), thank you, Felipe Lopez, for jump-starting my newspaper reporting career.

My pay for that huge, first-of-its-kind, exclusive? A whopping $150. One hundred and fifty bucks, or a little under one-sixth of my rent that month. Yes, I lived that dollar-to-dollar existence. For ten years!

As a result, though, Gallo assigned me two more college basketball articles, one on Fordham's team and one at the preseason NIT tournament. But I just didn't have the passion for it. I wanted to be around badass warriors, not college kids.

I then proceeded to do something that, to this day, I can't believe I had the balls to do. I went to Greg Gallo, even before I had the college basketball full-time gig, and I asked him for a promotion. "I know my limitations as a man," I told him. "I'm gonna fuck up one of these wiseass college basketball kids if they catch me on the wrong day. I need to be around men. Put me on the NFL—I will bring you so many back-page exclusives, you won't even know what to do with them." Shit, if you can't bet on yourself, who the fuck can you bet on? I pushed all my chips into the center of the table.

His response? "The NFL? What are you crazy? You have *zero* writing experience. That's the biggest beat in the world. I can't give you the NFL. You just don't have enough experience."

Well, I certainly misjudged that one, didn't I? OK, it was time to readjust. As you can tell, I already had plenty of experience in getting turned down. But even then, I had zero experience in staying down. Every single time you are knocked down, figure out an adjustment. If you're in war and your gun doesn't work, you can't just call a timeout. You need to adjust, or it's your life and the lives of your teammates. During the pandemic, when our businesses and schools could no longer meet in person we had to adjust to virtual meetings. It's the same in life. Don't take their version of "no" for an answer. Adjust, and then re-adjust, and then adjust again, until they say yes, until you figure out a solution that works.

So, I adjusted, even though my adjustment basically prevented me from getting my first ever full-time job. "OK, if it's experience I need, I will go out and get a ton of experience, and I will come back to you in a year to cover the NFL," I told Gallo.

Seriously, what fucking world are you living in, Glazer?!? But in my mind, it made sense.

So, that year, I got gigs writing radio spots for Bob Costas for $10 a jingle (that too was through David Blatt, the CBS producer who got me the fifty-bucks-a-game tape-logging job). I picked up experience writing for all sorts of magazines as a stringer. I did every radio show on the planet that called and needed an "NFL or Giants or Jets" guest. I even turned to the other reporters in the Giants' press corps who, by this time, had started to cease their ripping on me, having realized I was there to stay. They appreciated how hard I worked for scrappings, and I picked all their brains, eventually making them my teammates too. I learned how to write ledes, how to format stories, how to tinker with my grammar, everything. Once again, I took my ego out of it, and I was, and remain willing to be, coached by anyone. Learn from anybody and everybody you can. A blackbelt could still learn from a white belt.

One year later, nearly to the day, I called Gallo back and came out of the gates with something that, even now, seems at the top of my list of outlandish asks.

"Hey, Greg, remember me? It's Jay Glazer. I'm ready for the job you promised me," I said, dead serious.

"What job?" he asked.

"Last year, you said I didn't have enough experience to cover the NFL, so I went and got a year of experience, so I'm ready for the job." There was a pause on the line.

"I didn't say I was going to give you a job. *You* said you'd go get experience and be ready for the job. There is no job! *You* said it, not me."

Ah, semantics.

"Greg, you have nobody who can do what I do! You're getting killed by Mike Freeman at the *New York Times*, Gary Myers at the *Daily News*, Bob Glauber at *Newsday*. This is the biggest beat, in the biggest market in the world, and you have NOBODY! I'm your somebody!"

Gallo laughed, clearly amused, and probably a little curious by now. "OK, write an example of what you can do that nobody else could ever do and send that over in the *Post* form, and I will take a look at it."

Bam!!! There was my opening. That was all I needed. And it was a stepping-stone to adopting the Unbreakable Mindset, which I practice and coach and will teach you later in the book, teammate. This part is called being relentless, absolutely fucking relentless.

But now I needed a story. I knew exactly where to go, and who to ask. Enter Tyrone Wheatley. Tyrone Wheatley had just as much to do with me getting my career start as Michael Strahan, David Blatt, and Steve Serby. Yep, Tyrone freakin' Wheatley. He was the former University of Michigan standout and Heisman Trophy hopeful, All-American in football and track in college, and eventually, the seventeenth pick of the 1995 draft, by the New York Giants. He was an absolute star in college, but he never really found his groove on that level in the pros, and his career in New York started off murky to say the least. But I garnered his trust among a media corps he often quarreled with. How? By giving him a second chance when he was acting particularly emotional and frustrated.

Wheatley had grown furious over his lack of playing time, and while I was interviewing him for a Q&A about something unrelated, he just started venting about anyone and everyone, including the Giants' fans. Many reporters would've been enlivened by this circumstance. I turned off the recorder.

"Wheat, I'm turning this off for one second," I said. "Don't pick a fight with fans. I know you're talking out of emotion right now, but you'll live to regret it. Don't fuck with New Yorkers. They aren't the reason for your lack of playing time, got it? Now, I'm going to turn this recorder back on, and if you continue and want these to be your quotes, I am absolutely going to print them. I just want to make sure they are your words from your heart, authentically."

Wheatley paused, exhaled, and continued the interview, without saying another thing about the fans. Later that night, he called me to say how grateful he was. He asked if I had printed what he'd said about the fans and said he wouldn't have blamed me if I did.

"Nope, I gave you my word," I told him. "I want quotes that are authentic. I didn't need to 'catch' someone in a moment of emotion when you play an emotional game."

He explained that he didn't actually feel that way about the fans—he appreciated them—and the truth was he had become frustrated with himself but was basically taking it out on everyone else. Had I printed it, and I would have if he'd kept at it when I turned the recorder back on, it would have likely ended his Giants' career that day. There would have been no coming back from the kind of emotional shit he was spewing.

After that conversation, Wheat talked to me about *everything* in that locker room. Trust! Loyalty! That's what I was building. And it was that trust and loyalty that allowed me to take my next step, the one that would forever change the course of my career.

A few weeks later, Wheatley confided to me another story, this one that he was playing on a fractured leg. He was asking for advice. He believed the Giants had misdiagnosed his injury at the time. According to him, they told him it was shin splints. He told me that he was going to sue the team. It was another rant; only this time, I said I would love to print it. But he told me it was off the record. To note: off the record, in my language, means *off the fucking record*. There's no way around that. Not every reporter lives by this code as strictly as I do, and I frequently push contacts to go on the record. More times than I can remember, I've convinced them, but other times I couldn't, and I've accepted that reality. This balance is all part of what I dub the Art of Trust. However, in this particular case, I appealed to Wheatley's empathy for how hard my journey and struggle to pay rent had been these last several years. I came back to him on this, one week later, after remembering my talk with Gallo.

"Wheat, I know you told me that was all off the record, but I need to use it for a test column nobody will ever see," I implored. "It's for a chance for me to finally get a paid job, from the motherfucking *New York Post* no less."

"Really? You can actually get a paying job if I let you use it? It's that big for you?"

"Yes, it's that big."

"Go for it, you have my blessing!" That's why I build these teams and communities, crews from all different walks of life. We lift each other up on so many occasions. Sometimes you lift them and sometimes they lift you, and sometimes we all lift each other. This time, Wheat lifted me. I wrote the story for the *Post* and proudly sent it over to Gallo. "Tyrone Wheatley says he's playing on a broken leg." Home run I thought . . . until it wasn't.

"What is this crap?" Gallo bellowed into the phone.

"THIS is what I can do for you that nobody else can do," I proudly declared.

"This can't be true. If it was true, everybody would know," he said.

"Exactly, Greg, *this* is why you need me. It is true and nobody knows . . . including all your reporters at the *Post.*"

Despite my excitement and conviction, he delivered a gut punch in the form of a line I will never forget. "Look, I appreciate your moxie kid. Thanks, but no thanks."

You appreciate my moxie? Who the fuck talks like that? What are you a private eye in a 1940 movie? *Yeah, see kid, I appreciate your moxie, see, but I'm takin a pass, copper.*

Are you shitting me? I couldn't believe it. Wheatley asked how it went, and if "we" got it. I was rejected once again, but I gave myself exactly one day to grieve, then went right back to my grind, my relentless pressure to get where I was meant to be. It felt like I was getting closer, even though I'd been passed over yet again. Fuck me, though, paying bills was becoming harder. By the way, this entire time when I was struggling, Strahan would, every once in a while, say, "Jay, let me loan you money to pay your rent. I know you're good for it. I know you'll eventually get a job, and you can pay me back." He did that only twice, because both times, I absolutely lost my shit on him. "Don't ever offer that to me again! I will never, ever, ever take a dime from you! Everybody else may but I will be one of the ones who never, ever, ever freaking does!"

To this day, that still rings true.

But the same day I turned Strahan's last offer down, news suddenly broke: Tyrone Wheatley just got placed on injured reserve for the Giants with . . . a broken bone in his leg.

Hours later, my phone rang. "Jay, Greg Gallo here . . . you were right," he said.

"I know I was right, Greg," I said, in a way that didn't seem as dickheadish as it does when I write it here.

"OK, you got the job, you'll cover the NFL for us. You'll write a column every Sunday. Go get a passport photo taken, and get it to us, because we are going to have your picture next to your column, and your first one will be on the back page of the [NFL opening weekend] Sunday edition."

What? Are you serious? I was beaming, and shocked. I wasn't used to people delivering positive news to me on the job front. Honestly, I was trying not to cry. But fuck, teammate, enjoy the emotions, whatever they may be. If tears are warranted, then let 'em flow. It had been five years since I'd started interning at WFAN, seeking paid, full-time regular employment. Five years of being rejected and not knowing where my rent would come from, or how I would keep my electricity on (it was cut off several times due to my inability to pay my bill). Five long, hard years. This was IT!

"Ummmm, Mr. Gallo," I said. "How much is the salary?" Notice, now, suddenly, it was *Mr. Gallo* when I was asking about money.

"Salary? Who said anything about a salary? You get $250 a column. You'll do it for the regular season, and we'll go from there. So, you get two-fifty a week. That's what it is."

Two hundred fifty bucks a week . . . Fuck me!

TEAMMATE, LET ME ASK YOU:

Who is telling you no? And the bigger question is, when someone tells you no, are you letting them make you feel like you aren't worthy? People can tell you, over and over, why you "can't" do something. I've heard it constantly, for years, both before and after success. Fuck them. I will show *myself* why I "can" do something, and if I do it enough, others will eventually see that I can do it too. Door closing in your face, as you hustle to build the career you dream of? Look at it this way: if someone closed the door on you and locked it in real life, would you just sit there forever, with the door locked? Fuck no, you would start to panic and do whatever it took to get that damn door open. Well, you don't have to wait to panic before you react with that same ferociousness, in your career, in life. When someone slams the door shut, react! Kick it back open, like your goals depend on it . . . BECAUSE THEY DO.

LOYALTY IS
A LOST ART

Ya know what $250 a week got me? Validation!

They say more money brings more problems. Well, damn it, I needed some more problems, then. (Though I would eventually learn, having been on both sides of the spectrum, that my wallet is not my antidepressant! It definitely helps on the bills front but, nope, it doesn't erase mental health battles. That battle is from within.)

I did four years at the *NY Post*, earning the shit out of my, wait for it . . . $9,000 a year. Even though it was a part-time gig, I viewed that as my annual salary there. Well, I use the term "salary" loosely because I only earned that in some years, when I had a great story every week, of the thirty or so weeks that I had a possibility of landing coverage—six weeks of training camp; eighteen weeks, including the pre- and postseason; and a few weeks around the NFL draft and free agency. And only when Gallo agreed to print them. The shitty ones, he told me to try again the next week. Those were some heartbreaking weeks. So yeah, I know what it feels like to have the air sucked out of me. Over those next four years I would go on to make a jaw-dropping $9,450 a year. Sometimes more, but that's what I could consistently count on. Where did that extra $450 come in? That came from NY1 TV. They eventually told me that if I could get myself to the Super Bowl each year, they would let me do three NFL Insider television hits from outside the stadium for $150 each. I was on my way!

I know I'm teaching you how I went from broke to unbreakable (and how you could too, teammate), but at that point, well, forget going "from broke to unbreakable." I just wanted to move myself up the financial chain from "deadass broke" to "kinda broke." In order to do this, I had to expand out from having just Strahan and the Giants and Jets locker rooms as contacts, to having my little mafia grow to every locker room in the entire NFL. That circle grew by the day. Same way I built up trust in those locker rooms, which I dove into in the last chapter, I used those methods to build up my network all throughout the NFL.

People I meet out in public ask me all the time . . . "Why does everyone talk to you?" What these same people don't realize is . . . they don't. Not really. For every single contact I have in the NFL, there are ten other people who turned me down when I called them, looking for a scoop, or just to build a bond. But I can give two shits about rejection. That's another superpower of mine. I don't give a fuck if you turn me down. Why? Because what good does that do me, to live in fear of something that hasn't happened yet? We can't hit a home run if we don't swing the bat. We can't win a fight if we don't throw a punch. Fuck it, teammate, might as well swing.

Unfortunately, as I got more successful, I realized I started to care about rejection, because I didn't want to lose my success.

I had reckless abandon in the early days, because I only had one way to go, up. When I started to rise up the ranks, I wanted to prevent falling back down, in any way possible. Going back to deadass broke was horrifying. That fear of losing the things I'd earned let the fear of rejection sneak in. So, I've had to train myself to remember to legitimately not give two shits if I get turned down. Ahhhh, what a gift to have.

To build my Glaze mafia, the first thing I did was call all my contacts and ask them to reach out to other people in the league to let them know they can trust me. I asked these players and coaches to deliver a voucher on my behalf. My vouchers would say stuff like:

"This guy is crazy, but he's the most loyal fucking dude on the planet!"

I cold called the entire league, blindly called everyone, introducing myself, looking to talk to anybody I could, ready to show them they could trust me. I called tirelessly, during all hours of the day/night/after-hours/wee hours. I called and called and called. The 10 percent who did take my call, and with whom I struck up a relationship, most of them, at the time, were on the bottom rung of the totem poles in the league. That was OK; it meant that we shared a common fight. We were all fighting our way up, and it's less lonely when you are walking the walk with others.

Many of those early bottom-of-the-rung coaching contacts, about thirty or so, eventually became head coaches, and nearly as many became general managers and/or team presidents. As far as learning information, the higher someone was, the more they had. Thus, those same contacts who used to share scoops with me, later on in life, they had way, way, way more inside information as they climbed. Who would you give that information to?

Reporters you just met . . . or a reporter who walked those early years with you, when nobody knew your name? As they grew in stature, they knew they could ask me anything, and I would shoot straight. Too often leaders get in positions of power and those around them tell them what they think they want to hear. I told them the truth, unabashedly.

My contacts and I grew incredibly loyal to each other over the years.

Loyalty is a lost art that we need to reintroduce and reestablish in the world. The key to loyalty? That it pays off for all those involved, and there isn't a timeframe on it. Loyalty is a constant, an *always*. That's because you can't be half-loyal in the same way that you can't be half-sober or half-faithful to your wife. You either are or you aren't. You can't be half.

Full loyalty involves a give-give relationship. In other words, we both give to each other and boost each other up and win. Notice I don't say "give" and "take." Help each other win. Equally. Not everyone knows how to show this kind of loyalty, so I lead the way and hope others catch on. The one's who don't . . . they aren't in my crew. The ones who do . . . I will swing for the fences for them as much I will for myself. That's who you want on your team, and the kind of teammate you want to be.

What do I mean? Let's take my relationship with Strahan. (Look, I know I use him a lot early on here in this book, but that's because I spent every damn day with the dude for the first fifteen years of our careers. And it's not like he was famous back then—he was trying to prove his mettle, just like me. I'm sure you have a Strahan in your life, if you look for them—someone who has the same values, work ethic, and, most importantly, sense of humor that you do, and who will walk the walk with you, through even the brutalist slog for as long as it takes.)

Strahan helped me win by selling my trust and loyalty to others. And even though he denies it, he made sure I always knew what was going on and led me to the right trails to go after a story, as long as, in his mind, it didn't hurt the team. But if he heard shit on other teams, he threw it my way, immediately. Conversely, our relationship paid off for him in ways others do not know. This is why he put up with my shit for all these years.

For example, he started the 2003 season struggling. He registered a mere one sack in the first three games. I could tell he was stressing as a result. So, knowing what makes Michael tick, I decided to start lying to him about what players on other teams were supposedly saying about him. I wasn't stretching the truth a little. I was flat out making up bullshit, just to get him all pissed off and riled up. I know exactly what buttons to push on my dude.

That thing known as the internet had just come out (I think it's going to take off one day). And as far as Strahan knew, I had used my 14.4 baud connection on AOL to scan other papers around the country. At least that's what I told him.

He was only two seasons removed from breaking the single-season sack record, but this year, he just was off track. So, before he was to play the Dolphins in week four, I made up the first of a month and a half of flat-out lies.

I came up with some shit that Richmond Webb, Miami's Pro Bowl tackle, said Strahan had lost his edge, or something along those lines. One night, while Strahan was driving me home from Giants Stadium, I "casually" dropped this doozy right in his lap, and ohhhh yeah, he completely blew a gasket.

The result that Sunday? He ripped off nine tackles and a sack. Soooo, you're welcome?

I did the same thing the next week, about the Patriots offensive tackle. And while I certainly enjoyed fucking with him, predictably, he lost it again. *BAM*, he used that anger to fuel his way to two sacks in that game.

The next game? I told him Jon Runyan (Sr.) of the Eagles called him soft to other players I knew on the team, and they would mock Strahan. That led to two sacks against Runyan.

For the next month I kept making stuff up, and getting under his skin, and for that entire period he just kept buying my shit. I would love to say this was the first true sign I could act, and that my five seasons on *Ballers* could be traced to this moment, but that line would be more full of shit than the lies I was telling Stray. I was simply enjoying seeing the fucker unravel, and quietly laughing my ass off, as he became a damn tornado over and over again. Over these five weeks, my made-up stories helped launch him into such a frenzy, he ripped off eight sacks and thirty tackles (a large number for a guy teams barely ran at).

It only stopped because a month and a half in, well, I told him that the Jets' tackle, Lonnie Palelei, who used to be Strahan's teammate with the Giants, had told people he thought Michael was the easiest guy to block in practice, and he wasn't shit compared to another Giants lineman, Keith Hamilton. So, during the game, an enraged Strahan slammed Lonnie, in the middle of the play, climbed on top of him, and yelled, "You think I'm not shit?!"

Unfortunately for my little charade, Palelei answered back with, "What are you talking about? I never said that!"

Actual conversation between the two while on the ground.

Uh oh.

After the game, Strahan ran over to me. "Hey, I was so pissed at what Lonnie fuckin' said I slammed him down during the game and jumped his shit, but Lonnie said straight out he never said that," he exclaimed. "Jay . . . did Lonnie actually say that?"

Ummmm, what? Can you repeat the question please?

"Jay?"

Ahhh, Fuck it.

"Nope," I admitted.

"What?? No?!" Strahan said. "Did any of those guys this whole time say any of it?"

"Ummmm . . . well . . . no."

"Not one of them?"

"By not one of them do you mean . . . ?"

"Jay, did any one of those guys say any of what you said they did? That's what it means!"

Oh, now that I got clarity.

"Nope, not one . . . oh, and you're welcome!"

Yes, Michael, you're welcome. By the way, my little ruse only propelled him to 18.5 sacks on the year, the second-best season of his Giants career. Once again, YOU'RE WELCOME!

So, I gave Strahan a bunch of shit, and he gave me the joy of watching him unravel. Ya see, it's always been a give-give. OK, OK, in all seriousness, it was a give-give because he got back on track, and it helped him turn that year around into one of his career years. In turn, he told that story to tons of players and coaches, each time getting them to realize I was definitely not your typical reporter. He built me up, and I built him up.

At the end of his NFL career, our relationship certainly helped when FOX wanted to hire him to join our team.

When we hired him at *FOX NFL Sunday*, it was me who put the time in, night after night, helping him transition into his next career. His first year, even though I needed to be burning up the phone lines every Saturday night, before our show, hunting for scoops, instead, for a couple hours each Saturday night, I sat with Michael and went over what he was going to say LINE BY LINE. Line . . . by . . . freaking . . . line!

I coached him in delivery, use of pauses, how to use his eyes to tell a story, everything. Oh, and according to him, I was a task master. As much as he established me in the NFL, I was going to make sure he didn't fail AFTER the NFL.

I also made sure I pounded one particular lesson into him week after week after week. (Every pro athlete who makes the leap into broadcasting, LISTEN to this advice, it pertains to ALL of you. Anyone who wants to tell your story and find an audience, you too.)

"I know more about the NFL than 99.999999 percent of the planet, but I will NEVER know more than you," I told him. "I know who is getting traded before you do, cut before you, a new deal before you, fired before you, but I will never know what it's like under a pile, to be in the middle of a QB controversy, to have my coach fired, to have teammates cut, to have game plans either work, or unravel, on game day. You do.

"So, every single time you go on the air, tell me something that Jay Glazer wouldn't know. If I don't know it and am learning, then the fans are learning too. So, don't give me stats or tell me some shit I can read in USA Today. Give me something that only a player would know, give me that insider perspective, pull back the curtain."

Then, I even went over how to deliver it with him. Literally, when to pause, how to not stumble, how to throw out repetitive phrases. If I have learned it, I can coach it.

Relationships are everything to me. They fuel all areas of my life and certainly made me rise in my career as a reporter. For example, I once broke a story that the Jets were going to trade the number one overall pick in the draft . . . the one and only Keyshawn Johnson. One day, out of nowhere, I got a call from a friend on the Ravens, a scout whom I had chatted up in the Giants Stadium press box at a game. He was one of those thousands of guys I had reached out to, and one of the minority that stoked the relationship back my way too. He called me out of the blue and said, "Hey, I remember hearing you and Keyshawn Johnson almost got into a fight." (Yep, he didn't like what I wrote about him one day. The pure ridiculousness of my response to his anger defused the immediate tension. Keyshawn and I actually became close after that. He laughed at it and, like those other early sources, told anyone who would listen that I'm batshit crazy. Hey, a little fight sometimes builds respect.)

Anyway, this scout asked me about Keyshawn's character and what his teammates thought of him.

"Why do you want to know?" I asked him.

"Because the Jets are shopping him to us and the Buccaneers."

"What??? No fucking way. He was their number one pick!"

"Jay, why else would I be asking you for this information? Nobody knows these guys like you do. Tell me everything you can about him."

Ya see? Win-win. I got a MAJOR, MAJOR scoop, which I broke all over the place. And this scout was able to go and tell the Ravens inside info on Johnson. Both teams were in it, and the Bucs out-bid the Ravens and offered more to trade for him than the Ravens, but it all made that scout look good.

Those relationships paid off in scoops I would never have imagined—major, crazy scoops for the *Post*, over and over and over again. Guys came to me because, as they said, if anyone was going to break it, it might as well be me. Like what you ask? Oh, how about this doozy . . . I met a guy who played wide receiver for the Cardinals at my first ever Super Bowl, which was in New Orleans. The next year the player called me and, well, very little shocks me, but this one did. He told me the Cardinals were cutting him, which seemed odd because he was a good player. When I pressed him, he point-blank and very truthfully admitted he was getting released because he stole checks out of his teammate's lockers and was cashing them.

"Ummm . . . huh?" I asked. What the fuck else am I going to say?

"Yeah, and I wanted you to have the story if anyone is going to have it."

Come again? I'd heard of guys stealing shit from other player's lockers, but I had never had someone point-blank drive the white Bronco right to the front door of the police station with me in the passenger seat, if you will. Imagine that *New York Post* headline? I don't remember what it was but it's these types of different scoops that started giving my name some sway in national reporting circles. I kept dropping crazy bombshells and my hope was that it would pay off.

Finally . . . after ten years of absolute suck, exhaustion, rejection, and yep, making a whopping $9,450 a year . . . June 1999, I FINALLY got "the call." The call I had been working so relentlessly for.

I was on the Randall's Island Golf Center driving range, with then-Giants running back Tiki Barber, when my phone rang. It was my agent, Maury Gostfrand, the only one who saw something in me after scores of others turned me down because I "would never be any more than a local New York guy." Or I "just wasn't good enough for them to see a future for me."

After a few seconds of friendly banter and "how are yous?" he said, and this is burned into my memory . . . word for fucking word . . .

"OK, you ready? You can exhale. We finally got you a full-time job offer!"

"WHAT? Are you serious? With who?" I yelled, shrieked, screamed, all of it.

"CBS Sports. *The NFL Today* on CBS. Congratulations, you are going to be their new NFL Insider."

I . . . started crying . . . right in front of Tiki.

"Don't you want to know how much for?" Maury asked.

"I don't give a fuck, I'll take it!" I exhaled and cried some more.

"Fifty grand a year, Jay," he said.

Then I cried even more.

I cried because in that moment, all my faith in God, in the Universe, and in myself came true. Here was the payoff of that day back in 1993, when I'd proclaimed to myself, "I will get to the top by being the last motherfucker standing, and I will out-work the world."

That moment with Maury . . . that was my moment that validated it all. Whoever said quitting isn't an option is a complete and total moron. It's the easiest option in the world. It sits on your shoulder every damn minute of the day.

There were ten years I could have quit. Ten fucking years of being rejected, turned down, rejected some more, turned down some more. Ten years of putting on a "happy mask," even after being ignored, or told "no," over and over and over again.

But the opposite is harder. Being the last motherfucker stand-ing is a full-time job that grinds you down and wears you out. That's where the lesson of this chapter comes in, teammate—on the days when your career is stagnant and flatlining, and you don't know how you are going to keep going, it's the people walking the walk beside you that give you strength. It's taking the time to have a laugh over a beer, with someone who's never given you a scoop, because they're good people. These relationships pay off every single day, long before the connections they weave into your life ever will. So, treat them like gold.

One week after receiving Maury's call, my new role for fifty grand turned into an additional job for another $50,000, when I became one of the very first minute-by-minute breaking newsmen in America. It was me competing for scoops, versus the great Len Pasquarelli, John Clayton, and Chris Mortensen of ESPN. Three days after that, I got a weekly gig with WCBS-TV in New York, for another $35,000. In the span of ten days, I went from $9,450 a year to a stunning $135,000.

Over the next five years at CBS, I broke some of the biggest bombshell scoops of the first part of that decade. Huge, monster scoops like the BALCO steroid scandal, Barret Robbins of the Raiders going AWOL before the Super Bowl, and the Raiders booting him from the team for the game. Washington, shockingly, rehiring long-retired legendary coach Joe Gibbs, the equally legendary Bill Parcells getting secretly hired to coach the Dallas Cowboys, the NFL's intention to start playing Super Bowls in cold-weather cities like New York . . . I broke a ton of huge scoops. That got FOX's attention. They offered me a contract, one minute after my deal had run out at CBS, which was after the Super Bowl in 2004.

I accepted and signed with FOX to do *FOX NFL Sunday*, sideline reporting, *Best Damn Sports Show Period*, and host the first ever MMA studio show in US television history, *The Pride Fighting Championships*.

That's where loyalty got me. Paid. The top of the hill. Validated.

But there's another lesson too, the final one of this chapter. This lesson is called "The Universe conspires to help us."

Let me explain: The first ever feature I did for *FOX NFL Sunday* paired me with Steelers Hall of Fame running back Jerome Bettis, who I'd become very close with over the last few years. Bettis allowed me into his house on Monday morning, to film him, literally, as he woke up, to show how long it took him to get out of bed, the day after a game. We played footage of him the day before, as I narrated, "This is the Jerome Bettis millions and millions watched on Sunday for the Steelers." Then we cut to me in his house, Monday morning, as he was icing both knees and trying to slowly get out of bed.

"But this is the Jerome Bettis nobody sees on Mondays . . ."

The feature was eye-opening, partly because of Bettis and partly because of my producer, who magically captured this rare footage and made it feel as raw and authentic as it was in person. It was my first-ever feature on national TV. First one *ever*. But want to know the even cooler part? Ready for a mindfuck?

That producer was . . . David Blatt.

Who? David Blatt . . . the same guy who met me as I walked off that stand-up comedy stage fifteen years earlier, and who gave me my start, with a job logging tape at CBS for fifty bucks a day. The very same David Blatt. How wild is that?

Ya see, teammate, the universe really does conspire to help us.

TEAMMATE, LET ME ASK YOU:

Are you as loyal as you could be? And here's an even tougher question, are you loyal to the right people for the right reasons? Not because you need something from that person, but rather, you just want a true bond. Remember, we're only interested in give-give relationships. That might mean letting go of some other people who aren't holding up their end of the deal. This is going to sound a little morbid, but the way I go about my relationships, I give the type of loyalty where I will end up being that person's pallbearer. I know, I know, a little morbid. But think about it. What can be a greater expression of loyalty than to be chosen to carry your loved one to the end? If I treat all my friends like this and even just 10 to 15 percent repay me with that same loyalty . . . that's a pretty damn cool crew I have to walk this walk with me. I try not to think about the other 85 to 90 percent who weren't as loyal back. I simply build and honor the group that was. Relationships are everything, so treat them like gold. BECAUSE THEY ARE.

3

LIVING IN
THE GRAY

an, I made it.

I'd climbed and climbed and climbed some more on my journey, busted my ass over and over again, even when seemingly insurmountable odds were against me, and now, all that hard work had finally paid off. Not to mention, since my success was in the form of a TV deal, everyone who'd doubted me or made fun of me along the way would now see me triumph—not why I'd been doing all this, but still sweet.

How about this? Four years after I joined FOX and shot that feature with Bettis and Blatt, I signed my second contract with FOX, which made me the first seven-figure NFL Insider, ever—a way different lifestyle than $9,450 a year. Then, in the next contract, I earned even more. And in the next deal, even more, and on and on.

Now, before your eyes glaze over, and you start thinking I'm just another out-of-touch guy bragging about my bank account, and I've got no idea of how hard you're struggling to reach a goal that's worlds away from a seven-figure anything, that's not the point of this story. What I'm trying to tell you, teammate, is that I basically bareknuckle boxed my way into my exact fantasy job, not by being the smartest or the best educated or the person with the best manners. As I've been teaching you all along, I did it with qualities that are within your power to cultivate—authenticity, hard work, determination, loyalty. And if you don't give up, you can do it too. You may be surprised to find this is true. I know I was—I already told you, I fucking bawled my eyes out. And now, I had actually done it, and even done more than I'd ever dreamed I would do.

I had established myself so much that, in 2017, I got cast as, get this, the affable yet over-the-top (but of course still-quite-lovable) character of Jay Glazer, for five years, on HBO's *Ballers*, with The Rock. Two years after that, my dream took my *FOX NFL Sunday* crew and me to an even higher peak. In 2019, we were the first ever sports show to be inducted into the Television Hall of Fame, mostly because of Bradshaw, Howie, and Jimmy, but shit, I think I pulled enough of my weight on the team. (As we're going to get into later, teammate, one of the best things we can do for ourselves is to brag and love ourselves up!) There I was, onstage, at an awards ceremony in Las Vegas, accepting a Hall of Fame trophy. The freaking Hall of Fame, people!

Brief sidenote: As we stood next to the stage, about to get our Hall of Fame awards, I turned to Howie Long and said, exactly this, "Hey, bro, I know we are supposed to act like we've been there before . . . but MAN, FUCK THAT, I HAVEN'T! This shit is COOL!" Howie started laughing at, and then mostly with, me. He was reveling in it too. But shit, for someone like me, who once had a freakin 2.4 GPA, who had to get turned down a billion times to finally get there, and who had been told

"You're not good enough" over and over again, this was the moment of total redemption.

I had made it, which, obviously, means happiness . . . doesn't it? How could I NOT be happy? That's what happens in the movies, the main characters struggle their asses off, they climb the mountain, overcome insurmountable odds, then reach the pinnacle, and there are these big, beautiful skies of blue, and rainbows and unicorns and pots of gold . . . all sorts of happy songs of celebration. Isn't THAT what it's supposed to feel like? I always thought if I went after my career with sheer force and reached my goals, I would be happy. Sounds logical, right?

Many of you have seen me in my loud moments on camera, all the smiles, all the laughs, and the whole time, while I looked like I was living it up, doing the "happy dance" on the outside . . . the truth is . . .

I was full of shit.

That "happy dance"? I honestly didn't truly understand what the word "happy" meant. On the outside, I was the life of the party, living the dream and laughing my ass off. But on the inside . . . fuckin' ay I was dying. I was dying because of something that I call THE GRAY.

Ahhh, the gray. The gray is why we are here, so I can teach you about it, and so we can learn how to beat it together, teammate.

The cornerstones of the gray are *depression* and his fucked-up twin sister *anxiety*. That's the world I live in behind my eyes.

But I don't want to simply leave it at that.

How can I best describe the gray? Living in the gray feels like an internal bleeding of the soul. Like my insides are a wasteland where no trees or flowers could bloom. It's suffocating, dark, bleak, lonely, and painful, mentally, physically, emotionally, and spiritually. There is no spot that feels good. Living in the gray makes me feel slow as shit. My body aches, but it's my feelings that hurt the most. Way beyond being thin skinned, I'm walking around with NO SKIN, all my nerve-endings exposed, or at least that's how it feels. My whole house, life, world, brain, is that nasty ass gray . . . not the Crayola gray that's kind of pretty, but instead, this dark, ominous gray. Disgusting gray. It's fucking disgusting! All of it.

If the first three chapters in this book described the "outside" Jay Glazer, the one who outworks the world, treasures and displays loyalty, and yearns to make you laugh, this chapter pulls back the curtain on what it's really like to walk the walk with me, while dealing with this shit.

Whether you live in the gray or not, the more you can understand its effects, the more you can also help identify with others who may be there, right next to you, right now, but are too afraid to say something. The pain and shame that cause many of us to hide the gray feel just as bad as the depression itself. The more you know about it and can understand those who live in the gray, the more you'll be able to be a better teammate, leader, coach, husband, wife, son, daughter, mother, father, coworker, etc.

Rather than just trying to spill a bunch of word vomit on these pages to describe the gray, let me explain it by repeating what I said to Los Angeles Rams head coach Sean McVay, largely considered one of the top coaches in the NFL, who if all was equal, players would choose to play for. (An important detail because it speaks to his integrity. If you live in the gray too, choose the people you open up to carefully, because they'll give your vulnerability a soft place to land.)

Two weeks before I sat down to write this chapter, I had

dinner with Sean and his star left tackle, Andrew Whitworth, while we were in Cabo San Lucas. (Sidenote: this dinner was one night before QB Matthew Stafford happened to check into the same hotel we were all at. Yes, people, totally by coincidence. I know it sounds crazy that we all happened to be there, but that's the truth. So, the night before, Stafford, Whitworth, McVay, and I had dinner, in what started the ball rolling to get Stafford traded to the Rams, just two days later, while we were on that same trip.) I actually told Sean in detail about life in the gray, exactly as I'm about to tell you. The same EXACT thing.

"Most of your players, they are dealing with some form of a darkness like this," I told Sean. "Not a few of them, Sean, but *most* of them. It's what prompts most of the guys in your locker room to be crazy enough to put a helmet on and smash their heads full speed into other men just like them, over and over and over again. It's what prompts someone like me to take three steps up into a cage, to willingly get punched in the face by Chuck Liddell. The more you can understand this, the more you will be able to relate to your team!"

"How many players in our locker room do you think go through something like this?" he asked.

"No, Sean, that's not the question you need answered."

"Huh? What do you mean? I thought you're trying to help me understand depression better?"

"The question you need to ask, to really understand this, is not 'How many of your *players* do you think have this?' It's so much bigger than that. The question you need to ask is 'How many people in your organization, your whole building, your social circle have it? How many people sitting next to you each day go through it, and you have no idea?' That's what you need to ask."

At first, Sean just couldn't grasp it. So I had my work cut out for me. But if the head coach of the Rams didn't fully understand it, a guy who's job it is to connect with everyone on his team and also make them all one cohesive machine, I thought, *How many others don't?* Why I love Sean was the fact that he actually sat with me to learn about it, partly to take a little burden off me, but also, to genuinely understand people like me . . . like many of you.

"I guarantee you, you've got coaches on your staff, scouts, team executives, secretaries, people you see smile every single day, and dude, you have absolutely no idea the pain they are covering with a mask, to hide it from you and everyone else. Imagine if you had an understanding, or actually, Coach, even just a better idea? If you can talk about it, if you can openly tell others around you that you now understand it more, imagine how much better a coach this would make you!"

Look, folks, I'm not a doctor, I'm not a therapist, I'm not a psychiatrist, I'm not clergy . . . I am just a guy who has lived his entire life in the gray. But I'm also a guy whom God blessed with the ability to communicate, so I'm going to use this blessing to help you and people like Sean McVay and everyone else. But in order to do that, I need to tell you—as I told Sean—the reality of life in the gray.

Then, I really, truly, explained to him what this shit feels like . . . just like I'm about to do with you. OK, deep breath, deep breath . . . here we go. Let's start with the depression part of the gray.

Let me say this as bluntly as I can . . . Depression is an asshole!

"Sometimes I wake up and just stare at the ceiling and start crying, man," I told Sean, as I watched his mouth literally drop open. "Why are you so shocked?"

"Jay, honestly, man, I've heard about depression. I've just never heard it described to me in detail. I'm glad you're telling me, but if we didn't have this conversation—" He suddenly stopped himself mid-thought, "Wait, you're telling me, you literally wake up and just start crying?!"

"Yes, Sean, that's exactly what I'm telling you."

"And you have no idea why?"

"Yeah, dickhead, I know why . . . because I have depression."

"No, no, no . . . good one, asshole," he said, obviously one to keep up with my lovable jargon. "You wake up crying. Is there a particular thing that triggers you? Like something you're worried about? Something that made you sad?"

"No, man, that's the shitty part. It doesn't come with a warning. It just wakes you up and hurts so fucking bad. It just fucking . . . hurts. I feel as if these imaginary chains start pulling me down, but pulling me from my soul, and they're pulling down with them any belief it can get better. Man, it just feels hopeless *and* helpless. Think of how hard that is for a dude like me, or one of your coaches or players, who are so used to navigating at a high level. Let me put it this way: Imagine if you entered every game knowing everything was against you. The worst things that can happen, you're just convinced will happen, and there ain't shit you can do about it. Even worse, you feel like all that bad stuff is going to happen because that's what you deserve to have happen to you. Even though you're better than that. You just don't expect anything good to ever happen.

"That hurt causes dark valleys, where your mind goes to the worst, sky-is-falling, scenario every time," I continued. "Everyone's against you. Your relationships don't make sense, so you start questioning them. Things become a big deal that really aren't. Your fuse is overly short. So relationships become harder. You're always sensitive. You feel like you're constantly under pressure, and you think everyone is against you. It's always, *this fucking person did this . . . that fucking person didn't do that!!*"

"Man, how can you even function like that?" he asked.

Now he was getting it. Great question, Sean. How do I?

I'm not sure how I function to be honest. I function because I have no other choice but to function and not let the gray win. But, man, it's hard. Depression has led me into a ring, and a cage, to fight other men. However, what I didn't admit to you earlier is that it led me to a ring, or a cage, not to win, but to actually take beatings, because that's what I felt like I deserved. My depression told me that was my self-worth. Think about how sad that is? I believed I deserved to get beaten in a cage, just because depression said so. Worst part is, I felt like I didn't have a voice against it. So, it did with me what it wanted. Sadly, I have learned to live with my abuser.

Sean and I continued to drink our cocktails as we waited for our appetizers, and I continued to peel back my own skin.

"Even though I KNOW I'm in a valley, I know I'm not seeing things right, I still can't separate what's real from what's not. Then, on top of the pain I already feel from depression, add to that the pain of guilt from lashing out. Then, the gray becomes absolutely disgustingly ominous. The unworthiness grows even heavier."

"But Jay, you have to know that's not true, right? You have to. I mean, look at your life!" he said.

"That's EXACTLY the problem, Sean, when you live in the gray, you don't see your life the way everyone on the outside sees it. No matter how much you say it, it's a struggle for me to see it.

"It actually has a fucked up schedule of its own too. Mornings can be hard, lunch time can be exhausting, sundown often feels bleaker, but my worst moment, the absolute WORST . . . every single day, no matter what, are those fifteen minutes when I lay my head on my pillow at night. Those fifteen minutes are TERRIBLE!!!!"

"Why is it worse at night?" he asked. I could see he was truly taking mental notes now. "Wouldn't that be better because you get to rest from it?"

"I wish! For many of us who live in the gray, we despise the feeling of being in our own skin. At bedtime, when you're stuck without life's distractions—it's just you and how shitty you feel, you are stuck with someone you loathe being around. For me at least, those are the hardest moments to endure."

"So, you actually *feel* it?" Sean asked.

"Yes, I actually feel it. Every minute of every day."

"Man, I am just blown away," he said.

Unfortunately, it is this feeling that leads many of us, yes, US, to drugs or alcohol, to numb and dull that pain of being stuck with someone, twenty-four/seven, who you just don't like, whose skin you hate being in. Led me to Vicodin and way too much alcohol. Vicodin is a painkiller, but the pain I used it for wasn't the pain it was intended for. Total transparency, I used Vicodin for eighteen years, at first for actual physical pain as a result of how beat up my body was from all the training in a cage . . . But then, I used it to attempt to deaden the emotional pain I felt every damn day and night.

"OK, so now that's the depression part of the gray, Sean," I said. "Unfortunately, there's more."

"What do you mean?" he asked.

Depression brings along an equally nasty partner in crime, its uglier, ever asshole-ier, twin sister, anxiety. Like depression, anxiety is a nightmare that brings a whole different set of problems. Here is something I have never told another soul . . . until now.

In 2005, in the middle of my second year at FOX, the "anxiety" part of living in the gray started affecting me on camera. Nobody who was watching knew, nor did anybody at FOX. But here's the ugly truth: since that week in 2005, I have suffered an anxiety attack every single time I have been about to go on TV, in the five or so minutes before you first see me on camera, and then, for an always-different amount of time while I'm actually on camera.

It's bizarre because I LOVE being on TV. I have zero fear of being on camera. Yet, like clockwork, every single freaking time I am nearing go time, I start sweating. Have trouble breathing. My eyes dart back and forth, and it's difficult to focus. My heart races like I'm about to have a heart attack . . . all this while, I'm standing there, waiting to talk to millions of you at home. I have no idea why these anxiety attacks started, but I have struggled to wrestle with them, and all these years, I've kept it to myself. I never told a soul. I'm sharing it now to help show others who suffer similar attacks that they are not alone. To show that even people like me, who seem to be crushing it professionally, can still battle anxiety attacks that show up whenever they damn well please. (And this is why, teammate, we have to make a pledge to be as vulnerable and transparent as we can. Because you never know who looks like they're at the top of the world but are actually dying inside. And if it's you who's been hiding how deep you are in the gray, when you dare to get real about it, not only will you help yourself by feeling less alone, but you'll also have the possibility of helping others to fight their own shitty demons.)

Anxiety shows up unannounced; doesn't need an invite. It

can really give two fucks about the worst possible time to pull up a seat and try to ruin everything. That's because it has its own calendar. It does not matter, nor take into account, if you're supposed to start a new job, go on a date, or have a meeting. It doesn't even care if it's THE BIGGEST DAY OF MY ENTIRE CAREER!!! And I'm about to be on the Super Bowl LIV broadcast team . . . on the biggest stage in NFL history.

Let me set the scene here. Super Bowl LIV, Kansas City Chiefs versus San Francisco 49ers, facing off in Miami. Not only was it the biggest game of the 2019 season, it also marked the one hundredth anniversary—the centennial season—of the NFL. (Hilarious side note, and yes, my ADD kicks in, no matter the seriousness of our subject matter: Right after the ball was kicked off to start that game, Terry Bradshaw turned to Howie, Strahan, Coach, Curt, Tony Gonzalez, and me and said . . . I shit you not . . . "This whole 'centennial' thing the NFL did this year worked great. They should think about doing it again next year." Dead . . . ass . . . serious. To which we all turned our heads in perfect unison with a collective, "What the fuck did you just say?" Yes, Bradshaw is THAT funny in real life without always trying to be. Twenty years from now, I'm pretty sure I will remember Bradshaw's line more than Patrick Mahomes's first-ever Super Bowl snap.)

Not as funny though, I spent the entire first hour of our Super Bowl broadcast on the biggest day of my career, negotiating with my gray to stop trying to choke me out, to let me be, to let me have my day. But it was no use. The anxiety stepped up its assault on me—for whatever reason it chose that day—and was worse than normal.

Come on, work with me here. Not on the morning of Super Bowl LIV! Please? Can't I just BE for one day? Not a whole day . . . okay, okay, you're the boss . . . we know that by now. How about just six hours?

I hate my abusers.

Don't pass out. Stay with it. I literally had to negotiate and coach myself into not passing out. Why? Because my anxiety said so.

After the first hour of our show, the anxiety attack suddenly stopped with the same randomness with which it appeared. Poof, magic. That's when I really step into my zone. *I love it here. I live for this. This is the only place I want to be.*

Two hours later, our group walked into Hard Rock Stadium and was introduced to the crowd and on TV for the whole world to see by the one and only DJ Khaled (another one of those "Mom, how the fuck did I get here?" moments)—to host the rest of the pregame show, leading right up to "God Bless America," the National Anthem, and kickoff.

I never told my teammates about my struggle that day. They won't know unless they read these pages. I didn't offer it up in the moment because I didn't want to make it their problem, to take away their happiness. And I didn't want to give the gray more strength in the universe. I try to protect my teammates from it as much as possible, because I don't want it to affect their happy place.

However, I'm not always successful in masking it. On one particular Sunday morning during the 2017 NFL season, we were meeting in what we call the Avocado Room (our official name for our Green Room inside FOX Sports). I was spinning out of control, with zero perspective, certain I was fucked. A self-sabotaging meltdown that came along with this constant recurring image and fear that I was going to lose everything. I would die alone, and my entire world was going to come crashing down around me, and nobody would care when it did. When we get into this fear, we try to sabotage, to speed up the process of losing it, rather than live in fear that we will eventually lose it. This fear leads to terrible decisions. That's what I mean when I wrote that I was "fucked."

"Hey, hey, hey, the sky is not falling," Howie Long said, as he pulled me aside and tried to get the roommates in my head to calm down. "What's going on? It's not that big a deal. It's really not."

As much as I love and respect Howie, on this particular morning I couldn't hear him; all I could see was that the sky was not only falling, but that everybody I knew was conspiring to make it fall on me. And when the sky *did* fall and crush me, they were going to be excited about it. Do you know how absolutely terrible that feels? To think that everybody in your life is against you . . . when they're not?

The shittier part was that this anxiety attack was actually brought on by an antianxiety pill prescribed to me to, well, *NOT have fucking anxiety attacks!* Meds for me are unfortunately a crap shoot. I've been on over twenty antidepressants and antianxiety meds in more than thirty years and, yeah, well, here I am.

If you'd been living in the gray for as long as I have, trust me, you'd be willing to try anything too. The gray goes back to my earliest memories. I was taken to a psychiatrist as a toddler. I started therapy as a little kid. There is very little I haven't tried. Sometimes those manic moments, like the one with Howie, last a few hours, and sometimes they last a day, sometimes, in the shittier times, one day stretches into a week. The conversation I had with Sean McVay came in the middle of a seven-day manic meltdown. Worse, they aren't always capped at a week.

And Sean McVay wasn't the only coach I've opened up

to about this. I've actually started to share with many in the NFL over the past year, and as a result, these same players and coaches I've had relationships with for inside information are now coming *to me*, seeking information or perspective on mental health issues.

Sean Payton, the head coach of the Saints, was one of those coaches. Last year, after a very, very deep, heartfelt talk we had had about life in the gray, Payton chimed in with a very vulnerable and powerful thought of his own.

"Hurt people hurt people," he said to me.

Wow!

Those words hit me square between the eyes.

Hurt people . . . hurt people.

He was so right.

Those of us who are hurt tend to hurt others in an attempt to take out our pain elsewhere, probably looking for our misery to have company. It's not fair—not to them, nor to us. The gray has made it hard to be my friend. That's a very painful line to type. I have no control over it. I have had public outbursts, some of them violent. I have called friends, bitching incessantly about anything and anyone, feeling that the world is against me. I have railed with complaints for endless hours about things that, looking back, are incredibly inconsequential. I've also gotten pissed at friends over things that I have built up to be a big deal, when in fact they had very little to do with me.

For example, on that very same weekend I had that conversation with Sean McVay, the very next night at another dinner, I got all sorts of pissed off at him . . . for no feasible reason. None. Zero. In my mind I felt he'd wronged me about something. I got mad at the entire crew we were with. That's why it's hard to be my friend.

And I know it's not fair to them, and usually, a short time after, I beat up on myself more for pushing my friends away, or for tarnishing their good times. I beat up on myself terribly.

Luckily, Andrew Whitworth, the Rams' captain and left tackle who was also present for this whole weekend sat with me, with Sean, and coming off this conversation about the gray the previous night, asked me what was truly wrong. When I was all over the map, Whitworth said, "Well, don't push us away. You are pushing us away by you being angry. We are your friends . . . don't push us away."

Think about that! Had I not had the conversation the night before, I'm not sure Andrew and Sean would have handled it this way. But ya know what? As I type this, maybe I'm not so bad. Despite me hurting myself, and in turn hurting my friends, with my outbursts and sadness . . . they are all still here, standing with me. Wow, I honestly didn't see this until I typed it here. Not sure why it took me writing this down to shift my perspective for me, but it has. All these years, they are still standing right here next to me. I must be pretty damn special after all, if they stick by my side, despite all of this. Hey, gray, turns out I am more special than I realized.

That's why, Strahan, I can razz him and play a million jokes on him, but man, he's been there with and for me, through all the ups and downs, peaks and valleys. And he's still my friend. He deserves massive credit for that. It's not easy to put up with all of this for all these years.

And Curt Menefee. In my eighteen years at FOX, I have pulled Curt into our dressing room on a regular basis and melted down to him about some shit that's bothering me. And in turn, he'll calmly sit there and talk me down and get me to be calm. Curt has become my de facto therapist (if we add him to the list, that'll make him one of the six rolling therapists I have going at any one time). That's a lot of patience.

That's why I make sure when Curt calls me for help about anything, I drop what I'm doing immediately. Same for a few NFL executives like John Schneider, the general manager of the Seahawks. Been friends with him since 1997 and as much as we talk about football, we've talked more about my mental health than anything else over all these years. Schneids (as he's called in the NFL), even when he's in high-level NFL draft or personnel meetings, when I text him that I'm struggling, he leaves the meeting and gives me an ear. So does his wife Traci, anytime of the day. Again, do you know how challenging that must be for other people?

But in turn, I have been a loyal "emotional soldier" for them. Same thing . . . anytime, anyplace. Constance Schwartz and her husband, Mike, and my friend/agent Maury Gostfrand . . . over the years I have gone to them in tears, horrified, full of the darkest gray of my life . . . and every single time they were there for me. Even all the executives and producers at FOX, I'm grateful for them always rolling with me and my mania.

Or take fighters like Jay Hieron, Ava Knight, Randy Couture, and Chuck Liddell. Over the years I've had many, many, many depression-fueled valleys around them, and none have ever jumped shipped. Couture has seen me throw a table at someone in a bar, among other things. He often proclaims, "Jay is fucking crazy, but I believe in him, so I am always there." I think when you bleed with other people, you actually become more vulnerable with them. We fight together, we bleed together, and we cry together.

Maybe I'm not so alone and unlovable after all. It only took me fifty-one years to see this. I've been doing the work all these years without having it really sink in, until this book.

And now, I had one more person I could confide in who truly made an effort to understand the pain in my spirit. After I finished telling Sean all this crappy, dark, disturbing truth about the gray, he didn't run away from me. Instead, he thanked me for opening his eyes about what people like us, who live in the gray, go through. For trusting him with this vulnerability.

Can you imagine that? Leaders of men are now starting to show a little vulnerability with an NFL Insider, despite the "dudely" world many of us live in. It's time dudes realize talking about this does NOT take away our Man Card. I want us to know it adds value to our Man Card.

But dudes just aren't ingrained to think that way. Yet, if we hurt our knee, or ankle or wrist, we go see the doc, we openly talk about "getting treatment" (that's what physical therapy is called in the NFL). Actually, players are fined nearly *ten thousand dollars* if they miss treatment. Ten grand! So why don't we do this when our heart hurts? Or our mind is off? Or our feelings hurt? You're not a wuss if you talk about your feelings! Do you look down on me for talking about it? Do any of you think I'm weak because I talk about it? I would think not, so don't view yourself as weak either, teammate. Vulnerability makes us bad motherfuckers. That's the narrative I am trying to shift with this book.

"Jay, wow, I never would have known, man. So, you literally don't remember that first hour of your Super Bowl show?" McVay asked during our conversation about the gray.

"Nope, none of it."

"Shit, well, I couldn't tell," he laughed. "But, man, this really gives me a different perspective to think about. I need to digest all this and dig deeper. I think you talking about it, Jay, is going to make a difference. If you didn't sit here with me like this, I still never would have known. Bro, I'm proud of you, for talking about it like this. Man, I think you'll help a lot of people, but I think it'll be really good for you too."

So do I, Sean. So do I.

It's time I start fighting back, time we all fought back. The gray has fucked with us for too long. But I'm done letting it ruin my life and all those "happy dance" moments I was supposed to enjoy but couldn't.

It's time to expose the gray, teammate, and time for all of us to see some streaks of blue. Let's stop running from it, let's grab each other's hands, and run right back at it, and make it run from us. It's time we all fight back against this shit that has occupied us for way too damn long. That fight starts right here, right fucking now!

I'm putting it out there, for all to hear, so we can beat this fucker TOGETHER.

Let's not just beat it, let's take away its power altogether, by seeing where it's actually *helped* us, motivated us, pushed us. Can you imagine how empowering it will be if we can take our own gray, our own fuckedupness, and use it to empower us, to lift us, instead of killing us? Let's use the gray and turn it around on its own ass. Even if you don't have depression, or anxiety, or any gray, you can be inspired by the fight others show against it and support them in their battles. The gray hates that! It's time we fight back. So, fuck it, let's pull off the gloves.

Oh, and one more note, before we start our journey and learn ways to beat the gray: two weeks after our talk, Sean called me. Guess what he did?

He actually talked someone he's close to into going to see a therapist. He saw, from our talk, that it's okay to not be okay, and even more okay for people to ask for help.

Over these next seven chapters I'm going to give you a road map, three pillars, a game plan if you will, on how we can all fight back against the gray.

TEAMMATE, LET ME ASK YOU:

Are you lying? And by that I mean are you pretending you're fine when you're really not, maybe because you don't want to be a burden? Or because you're scared to admit to others—or even yourself—how fucked up you feel inside? As you've just seen, the problem with these lies is that they don't just hurt you. They also hurt the other people who could be helped by your vulnerability. So, try this: The next time someone asks you how you are, if you're having a shitty day, don't just say "Great!" Dare to say "I'm actually having a rough time today. Thanks for asking." You might go into more detail about why. Or you might not. Either way, you've just done something totally badass. You've been authentic! Now, try stopping and asking someone how they are, especially if they look like they could use a teammate. And don't just take the easy answer. Dig deep. BECAUSE THAT'S WHAT TEAMMATES DO FOR EACH OTHER.

BE OF SERVICE

Giants Pro Bowl running back Tiki Barber and I walked past the litter and empty crack vials, our breath steaming out of our mouths, and into the stairwells of one of the public housing buildings, deep in Harlem, NYC. Graffiti scrawled everywhere. People were lurking in the shadows, selling, buying. Yet instead of being fearful, I was getting the warm and fuzzies inside, just thinking about these children upstairs, and the surprise they had no idea was coming for them.

We climbed the stairs, found the door we were looking for, and knocked.

"Who's this?" the person behind the door asked. She gazed suspiciously from behind the security chain at this unannounced dynamic duo—a foul-mouthed, short, stocky, Jewish guy and a suave football player—standing on their doorstep.

"SURPRISE! Santa sent us!" I said.

"What the—?!?!" came the voice.

"Yeah, Santa sent us," Tiki chimed in.

"Your daughter sent a letter to Santa, asking for a new pair of shoes, and a jacket for her and her baby sister?" I yelled through the door.

"Yeah . . . oh my God . . . yeah," the person said, now realizing what was happening.

You can probably understand why they'd never thought, in a million years, that anyone would ever just show up and help them, letter or not. Much less the starting running back of their hometown Giants. It was incredible to see the looks on their faces as we were invited into their apartment, their eyes as wide as donut holes. They couldn't believe it!

These moments of giving were pure magic, so much so that it became an annual tradition for me, and I always got a hit of joy from those children's faces. But even though I was helping them, really, I was doing my Santa routine for myself.

It's called . . . Being of Service!

The first of the three weapons we'll launch against life in the gray is truly brilliant in its simplicity. It's something we can all do, rather easily, in fact. You decide how much time to put into it. It doesn't have to hurt your bank account, and it doesn't involve a single medication, doesn't have one lousy side effect. But it is a powerful way to come out swinging, in this massive brawl we are waging against the gray.

That's what had led Tiki and me to these public housing projects throughout NYC. It was December of 2001. Holidays were approaching, a time that can be especially difficult for many people, whether or not they have depression. It's a particularly nasty time for me because my birthday is the day after Christmas. (I call my birthday Glazemas, just to piss off my friends with how ridiculous it sounds. I come bursting into rooms, "Ten shopping days to Glazemas . . . what have you bought me?")

Even though I can laugh about this in the space of these pages, the truth is that for many of us who live in the gray of depression, birthdays are hard, because we don't have a grasp on how to celebrate ourselves. It's difficult to like ourselves, much less celebrate ourselves. In turn, it's just as challenging to feel worthy of letting others celebrate us. Then, the stress I feel because I can't celebrate myself brings on guilt, which just makes me feel even shittier.

Anyway, back to the story: someone had told me that the letters kids write to Santa are often brought to the post office, where they are sorted. I decided to go to the big post office in Manhattan, zip code 10001, and request some of the letters, to see if I could give any children what they'd asked Santa for that year. What I didn't expect to find was thousands upon thousands of letters, nor how incredibly heartbreaking many were.

Letters like: "Dear Santa, I am eight years old. All I want for Christmas are shoes without holes, so the other kids stop making fun of me, a jacket for my little sister, and so my mom stops crying at night, because we have no dad." Or: "Dear Santa, please give us a blanket, so my baby brother and I can be warm together at night." Or: "Please, Santa, I just want to have a jacket for each of us, so my mommy could feel like a good mommy."

Holy fuck, people!!! Talk about heartbreaking, gut-wrenching, and every other emotion you could throw into a bag. Wow.

The first year, I started with three letters. I went out and bought exactly what was on these children's lists: shoes, jackets, pants, shirts, blankets, and added in a Barbie and/or some toys. I bought things a kid might hope to find under the tree, and I included gifts for the parents as well, and it didn't crush my bank account. As the years went on, the number of letters I fulfilled grew. Which meant that I needed help. I recruited my

MMA fight team, the more the merrier. I knew once they saw those kids beam with surprised happiness, the gratitude would flow. Finally, I recruited Tiki, who jumped at the chance.

Eventually, my annual trips to the post office ended with me leaving with more and more letters each year, as friends asked if they could get some too. They didn't have a fight team to go into the projects with, so they fulfilled them and mailed them to the families with letters back from Santa.

I actually wanted to go in person. I needed to see those family members' joy firsthand. I never worried that I didn't have money to afford these gifts, even though in the first few years, I really didn't! I knew this act would pay itself forward . . . I was investing in the soul of the universe if you will.

Now, I realize you're probably reading this story and thinking, "Well, I don't have an NFL player to show up with and deliver gifts. Who do you think you are?" And it's true that you may *not* have an NFL player to shlep around with you, or a lot of money to spare. But that's where this unconventional antidepressant is so amazing.

You always have something to give: your time, your assistance, your advice . . . even just your smile. Oh, and before you go and start busting my nuts for being a cheese ball, I'm being totally sincere. We've got to stop being too-cool-for-school about this stuff. We, dudes especially, must stop worrying about being all macho. Showing vulnerability is tougher than going ten rounds in a ring.

Being of service does not have to be a monetary thing. For example, here's another way you can help others: TALK ABOUT YOUR ISSUES! Open up and tell someone, anyone. The more you can open up to others, the more it may help someone who you have no idea needs to feel like they aren't alone in whatever struggle they may have. You just never know who you're going to help. There is no shame in not being OK. You will see me say this a few times in this book. It's OK to not be OK. So open up to others so they can feel they aren't alone.

For example, you're already well-acquainted with my depression and anxiety. So, how's this for a kicker? On top of these ugly, constant companions that have been with me since I was a little kid, I was diagnosed with attention deficit disorder (ADD) at nineteen.

How can I explain ADD to those who don't have it? Hmmm, hold on, wait . . . what was I just talking about? (Hey, I can make the jokes . . . I'm the one with AD . . . shit, what was that last letter again?) ADD feels as if I'm watching five movies, having twelve conversations, and listening to four podcasts, inside my own head, which means there is zero room to focus on anything that's going on outside my own experience. For example, if I'm at a restaurant, I'm looking at the person I'm with, but I will still hear EVERY conversation in that room. In my head, I'm continuously being bombarded with sounds, words, info . . . until I have complete sensory overload. It's exhausting.

My brain, because of the ADD, doesn't see things in the same alphabetical order as everyone else. By now, I'm used to it. I try not to get bent out of shape. I try to find the power in it. That's why I'm so vocal about how what makes us different is our superpower . . . because we need to find that win somehow. But back when I was a kid, my version of being different was a total nightmare, especially because for years, nobody knew what "was wrong with me." In school, sitting still for an entire class was excruciating. Beyond painful. Every so often, I caught myself, wanting to listen to whatever the teacher was talking about, but I'd already missed so much, way too much. Trying to grab onto the pertinent facts as they whizzed by was like trying to leap onto the side of a speeding bullet train. By then, I was lost, and on top of that, pissed off. The inner wrestling match would begin: *Do I try to piece together what is being said, in order to catch up, or will it feel better to not even bother to try?*

Problem is, I was thinking about this internal brain teaser of mine instead of listening to the teacher . . . *again.* So, I'd become even more lost, with even less chance of catching up. More often than not, I'd give in to my ADD and attempt to find a distraction from the pain of being so far adrift from everyone else.

I didn't want to be a C-minus student. I didn't want everyone to think I was stupid. I didn't want notes getting sent home to my parents about my inability to concentrate, my bad grades, and the automatic judgment, "Jason doesn't apply himself." You know why Jason didn't apply himself? Because your teaching styles weren't conducive to all of us! One thing I have learned as a coach is that a single coaching style does not fit all fighters. But because I couldn't learn the way they thought I should, because of my ADD, they labeled me as having a "learning disability."

I absolutely fucking despised that label, that bullshit idea, that those of us with ADD have a "disability." To all of you "doctors and scholars," who labeled us that way . . . do you have any idea of the stigma you dumped on people like me? I may not be able to sit and "learn," via your horrifically boring way of teaching children. But demonstrate with a hands-on approach or coach something to me, and I guarantee, I will pick it up faster than anybody else. Shit, demonstrate five things to me at once, and I will pick them up faster than the average person. At the same time, if I coached you with my coaching style, which does *not* include sitting in a tight, overcrowded desk for one to three straight hours, getting lectured at, you would probably be at a disadvantage as well, simply because you happen to be wired to learn the conventional way.

The difference between us? I would not label you learning disabled because of it. I would realize instead that I need to find a better way to coach you. Simply putting a blanket label on someone and throwing meds at them (I was put on four different ADD meds beginning in 1989) isn't exactly being a great coach, is it? If that was my approach as a coach, I would be fired, and likely sued.

So, this is one of my ways of being of service, to explain what ADD feels like and the challenges those of us who have it face. For those of you with children who are dealing with ADD, for those of you who have battled this and been "labeled" as having "issues" because of it, I hope my speaking up is of service to you all. It's so powerful, because even just being open about our own struggles is a true gift to others. And one that has an immediate positive impact. THAT makes me see some blue . . . and I didn't need to spend a dime to do it.

Find something that touches *your* heart, teammate, something important to you personally and donate a few hours each week, or every other week, or every day, whatever your schedule allows. Just like playing Santa in the projects, the gifts are for others, but the returns are for you, the giver. This small investment will return significant streaks of blue. The more blue, the better we do.

Let me float a few more ideas by you on how to be of service to others. It doesn't have to be through an official charity or organization. Back in the '90s, living in New York City I kept walking past the same group of homeless people every day. One day, I just decided to stop and start talking to them, just strike up conversations, with the ones I always saw and knew were mentally stable. I always made sure I asked their names, because I figured when was the last time someone asked them that question? Just doing so, I hoped, gave them a little more personal enrichment, the feeling of being seen.

Stopping to talk to a homeless person and asking his/her name . . . that cost me zero dollars. By the way, the people I met doing that? Oh . . . my . . . goodness! The hearts I've seen. I once stopped to talk to one guy, who told me he was actually only on this corner to talk to other homeless people, because he used to be homeless and wanted to help by teaching them how he got himself off the streets. Here he was, being of service in the most amazing way, and I got to listen to and appreciate the joy in his voice. Many of these conversations helped me more than my weekly therapy sessions. When they brought me into why they were homeless, it was eye-opening and gave me perspective and gratitude, knowing I was helping to lift up a person.

Eventually, I decided to take my service a step further and start asking if any of them wanted jobs. When people said "yes," I gave them my time and helped them to find a job. You never know how hard people's struggles are. Landing homeless individuals a job was quite the uphill battle. For starters, they needed a home address. Obviously, that was impossible, since they were, ummm, HOMELESS. That was the point of this whole undertaking in the first place! They also needed a social security card, a phone number, and a bank account. I'd been ignorant of all this, and I was floored. (By the way, and we will hit this later, I have personally employed several homeless combat veterans in the last five years, and I made it much, much, much, much easier on them!) But back then, the challenge only helped me feel even more of service. I felt very little gray while figuring out ways around these hurdles. These were the days I was working for both the NY *Post* and NY1 TV, so I was known around the city, and I tried to use my swagger to talk to managers at fast-food restaurants, stores, studios, wherever I could.

Finally, on a Tuesday afternoon when I didn't have to go to Giants Stadium because it was the players' day off, I found a manager at a Burger King on the Upper East Side who had compassion and empathy, and who worked with me on putting my words into action.

"This is James, he's homeless," I told the manager. "I'm getting him on his feet. He really wants to work."

The manager allowed me to use my address and phone number, and I actually went and opened bank accounts with and for the homeless people I was helping. (Oh, by the way, I went to Times Square and bought them fake ID's, so we could open the accounts. Hey, I said I was trying to help, not win an award for most law-abiding citizen.) The manager met me halfway and kind of looked the other way, knowing it was my address and phone number on the application. Together, we got James everything he needed. And then, Burger King actually hired him!

The grand total of what I spent to help a man like James? Six dollars for the subway for us, $30 for the fake IDs, and $50, or so, to start a bank account—$86 in total to try to change someone's life. And for me, $86 to cut through the gray for a while. A much better value than what I was paying for antidepressants, antianxiety, and ADD medications. Yep, a bargain at half the price.

Of course, you want the payoff of the good deed you are trying to do for others, but equally important is the joy in the acts themselves. James and the others said nobody had ever made this much of an effort with them, for anything, in years, and it made them feel more . . . human. Wow, talk about melting my heart. Yeah, gray, try to stand up to THAT line!!! Other people's gratitude, it's a battle axe against that shitty gray.

I am not revealing all of this so that you say, "Gee, what a good guy Glazer is." Quite the opposite; I'm telling you all of this because I NEED to do these things, because my gray doesn't let me feel good about myself.

Being of service comes in all forms, and in ideas big and small, and again, it doesn't have to cost a lot of money to make it invaluable for both the other person, and yourself. I wanted to impart this lesson to my son, Sammy, too. I wanted to be of service to others AND to him. Twice a year, we go to the 99 Cents Store and buy toothbrushes, toothpaste, deodorant, wet wipes, socks, gloves, Band-Aids—thirty of each—and bag them up. (I call them our "essential bags.") Then I add in any clothes I don't need anymore. You can seriously do this for $200, plus the chance to clean out your closet. Then, together, Sammy and I drive around and hand out these bags to those in need.

"Hey, do you want some help?" I'll ask these total strangers.

Sometimes, they don't. Or they're not in a place to take assistance, because of whatever drug addiction or mental health issues they're dealing with. But frequently they might be a little surprised, since no one usually offers them anything like this, and will accept the offer.

Now, I know that some of you might feel weird or insecure about doing this. Most of us aren't necessarily equipped to deal with someone on the street who's in severe psychiatric distress. Sure, I've had people scream at me. I've had my offer rejected a ton of times. But that's all right; I know my truth. I know my intentions are good. I can withstand an awkward moment in the name of doing good for someone who really needs it. I mean, I tried to give a homeless man a turkey once, and he said, "No, I'm good, I'm vegan." Only in Beverly Hills, right?! But that's cool with me . . . at least I offered.

And the payoff I receive in sharing those moments with my son is absolutely priceless. After we finish making our deliveries, we'd sometimes take another lap around, and my son would spot someone we'd just helped. "Look, Daddy! Daddy, look, look, they're using them!" he'd yell out. Think about the cyclical effect of this action—not only are we being of service to others but I'm also aiming to instill empathy and values in my son that I hope he will take with him into adulthood, to help others and to help himself. Doesn't cost me a lot, financially, but it creates priceless moments.

OK, let's keep going here with ways to be of service. I am trying to list what I've done, hoping it can give you ideas, or jump-start your passion. I have done a lot, not to be Jason Teresa here, but because I have needed it. I didn't suddenly come up with Being of Service when I decided to write this book. Fighting my depression and anxiety is a daily and nightly battle for me. It's the longest round of any fight I will ever have in my life and there's no bell to give me a break. Well, let me take that back, there's no bell to end the round and give me a break by itself. Being of Service and the other pillars I will hit on in this book, they give me a chance to pause and catch my breath.

This is a call to action to step up and join me, teammate. Make a plan, right fucking now, for something you can do to help someone else. You don't need any special skills or training, just use what you have, use what you know. For me, that happens to be the NFL.

Back in 2003, I started a service project that lifts me up to this day (when I'm really struggling, I sometimes stop and make myself think about the stories I am about to tell you, in order to prevent myself from plunging into a tailspin). It was called Touchdown Dreams, and it was like Make-a-Wish on steroids.

In Touchdown Dreams, I started using my NFL connections to help children who were fighting for their lives. I'd find out what their favorite NFL teams were, and I would line up certain players and coaches to walk the walk with these kids. It wasn't a one-shot deal. I tried to link them together, so the kids felt they had that team supporting them throughout their battle.

I would send the kids to a team, and the head coach would make them captain for the day. Star players would take them to practice, give them wristbands or jerseys, then bring them inside for lunch with the team. Sometimes, they would go up to the head coach's podium. On game day, I would send a limo for the child and his whole family to go to the game—complete with sideline passes, the whole nine yards.

Andy Reid, then head coach of the Eagles, got a kid his own Eagles jersey, and we planned to have that child walk the team out of the tunnel at their game. Unfortunately for this boy, who was battling leukemia and had to have his hip replaced at an early age, the effects of radiation become too much for him on that day. So we used the limo to rush him to the hospital. After that, the Eagles kept up with him.

Wait for it . . . wait for it . . .

Not only did that boy make it through that episode, but he bucked the odds and beat the leukemia, which at the time seemed like a long shot. Years later, his father reached out to tell me his boy not only survived, but he made it to college and was an amazing starting pitcher for a college baseball team in New

Jersey. And how about this? He told me that it was the connection we made between him and the Eagles that had helped his son fight through those rough days.

Yup, cue Glazer freakin' crying again.

One kid, who I sent to the Chiefs, was on dialysis by age fourteen and was displaced from his home in New Orleans after Hurricane Katrina. That week the Chiefs were playing the Titans. I asked Herm Edwards, the head coach of the Chiefs at the time, to truly make him feel like he was a part of the team. And then, on game day, the Titans walked across the field and presented him with the ball as well. How freaking cool is *that*?! He started to cry. His mother later called me and gave me the shock of my life. She told me they thought he was born without tear ducts as THAT was the first time in his life he had ever cried. Can you imagine? And, yup, he cried, she cried, and then of course I cried . . . again.

There are many stories like these, and each and every one of them is special in its own way. It meant a lot to me to be able to use my connections to give back like that. And everyone in the NFL I approached was more than happy to help. Like I said, I think a lot of times, people want to be of service. They're just looking for a person to show them how. I'll bet there are connections in your own life that ONLY you can make . . . be that bridge.

Ask yourself what resources you have available to you at work, or through your own passions and hobbies. Figure out who needs what you have to give. Find a way to get it to them. Enlist your peers to help you, empowering them to be of service as well. Again, it doesn't have to involve a huge outlay of resources to make a big difference. If you work at a coffee shop or restaurant, is there food being wasted that could feed those in need in your area? If you're an organizing whiz, is there a local nonprofit that could use office help?

Finally, teammate, I leave you with a very, *very* important part of the process: love yourself up for your service, whatever it is. Let it sink in. Don't minimize it. Be fuckin' proud of yourself!! Love yourself up because you deserve it. Make it a new habit.

Every time you do something, however small, view it as big. Because it is. It all has a ripple effect. You may have helped someone, or you may have, without knowing it, saved someone. Maybe you did something for somebody, and because of that they had a better day, and then, they turned around and did something to lift someone else, who was in their darkest place. You never fucking know!! It really and truly all helps. Suddenly, it's expanding exponentially, until hundreds, then thousands, of people are finally getting the help they need. So, love yourself up when you do something of service for others. You did good!

Oh, and don't worry if the full positive impact of your service isn't immediately obvious. Trust that it's worth doing, no matter what. Trust that life is full of so many twists and turns that it will undoubtedly surprise you down the road, by revealing to you that you helped many others in ways you never could have predicted.

The ripple effect of being of service, that too may lift up tens, or hundreds, or even thousands, or millions of people. I knew I started Touchdown Dreams to help these kids fight the battles in their own lives, and in turn, fight my own battle against the gray. What I didn't know is that it would lead to a completely different movement. One little boy, a young leukemia patient named Logan Nobriga, who I took under my wing in his fourth year of an eight-year cancer battle, changed everything. All because I needed to be of service . . . The story of what Logan eventually led me to was so wild, and changed my life so profoundly, it needs to be told in not one chapter, but these next TWO chapters.

TEAMMATE, LET ME ASK YOU:

When was the last time you loved yourself up for something you did for someone else? (And if you can't remember the last time that you did something for anyone, this is a great moment to be of service!) But I'm sure there's something. Maybe when you got your afternoon coffee, you grabbed one for your colleague. Maybe you played soccer in the yard with your daughter for an hour after work, even though you were tired and had a report to finish. Maybe you donated $50 to save the whales. Or $5. Maybe you held the door for someone at the bank. Now, be proud of yourself. Remind yourself, in that moment, you made the world a better place, and hopefully you inspired that person to pay it forward. BECAUSE BEING OF SERVICE NOT ONLY HELPS OTHERS . . . IT HELPS YOU TOO!

THE BIRTH OF
A MOVEMENT . . .
THE MVP WAY

Twenty-two veterans kill themselves . . . every . . . single . . . day. TWENTY-TWO!!!! Let that number sink in. That is not okay. It is absolutely heartbreaking. Gutting.

Logan's battle with leukemia is also heartbreaking, gutting. Believe it or not, these two actually tie themselves together in a magical way . . . the last thing you probably expected to read. You will see what I mean over these next two chapters.

But back to our vets. Twenty-two . . . it's just not freaking okay! However, the number of combat veterans in our Merging Vets & Players (MVP) foundation who committed suicide from 2014 to 2019, our first five years of existence, when we expanded into five major cities? Zero!!! Fucking Zero!!! Not fucking one!!! Making this even more incredible is that many of our MVPers, before joining MVP, attempted suicide, many of them multiple times. THIS, this is a major reason I am writing this book. This paragraph right here.

When I first met my literary agents at an event for my

friend's book launch, they approached me and couldn't figure out exactly who I was or what I did.

"You're an actor on a sitcom but also work with the military?" a confused Jan Miller asked me, only to be more confused when another of her clients Dr. Phil, yup THAT Dr. Phil, stepped in and asked what his Dallas Cowboys were going to do with the contract of their star quarterback Dak Prescott.

"Wait, you're in football?" she asked. "I'm so confused."

"Yes, of course he's in football, but don't you also do something crazy like fight with those players?" asked her friend and my other lit agent Lacy Lynch. "But why was someone else here talking about you and Demi Lovato training?"

"I watch you on Sundays on FOX but were you in the military too or have something to do with the military, like you're working with veterans, or did you serve?" asked Carrie Thornton, the third member of their jolly little triumvirate, a senior editor from Dey Street, and the person who pushed this book into existence.

"Nope, I didn't serve . . . but I now serve *THEM*," I said.

All of them were officially and spectacularly puzzled. Shit, even I'm confused each day about what the fuck I do. But it wasn't until after I colored in between their blurry lines, then shifted to telling them about the lives I'm now saving and empowering with MVP that they all said, "Oh my GOD we HAVE TO do this book! You can save so many lives if we do this book. You have to do it, and we have to do it with you."

So here we are . . . together. The other entertaining stories??? They are simply a lead up to this. My tales of depression are to show you why I am unfortunately "qualified" to talk on this subject. Our MVP sessions are closed, raw, vulnerable sessions, but my crew has agreed for me to share our experiences and lessons in these pages in order for us to *be of service* to others. They all still want to be of service, despite their uniform coming off, and this is a way they can still serve their country, while serving their teammates (and that includes you).

I am writing this book because the lessons we teach each other in MVP have led to a massive transformation among our group of veterans, a high-risk group. I am hoping that what we use in our closed circle can help change the narrative on suicide, depression, and self-worth in this country, and this book can make a dent in that suicide epidemic. That is my hope, that is my dream, that is OUR mission together. This, teammates, is where we all truly get to walk the walk together. Anything and everything you read in these pages, I would hope you would pass along to others, those in need. And those who don't seem to be in need, well, you truly never know who looks like they aren't but are dying on the inside. As one of our vets, A. J. Perez, US Navy, eloquently stated in our closed group, "It's the invisible wounds that hurt the most."

It's time to heal.

But before we get into the lessons of MVP, I need to tell you about the birth of MVP, how this foundation, which I now call a movement, came to life. Logan was a big part of it, yes, and we'll get to his incredible role, but there's a lot more to the story. First, a phone call that completely opened my eyes and changed the course of my history:

"You've got to do something about your boy," said the wife of one of my NFL-player friends.

"Huh? What am I supposed to do? I heard he has pneumonia, right? I'm not a doctor," I replied into my phone.

"No, Jay, he doesn't have pneumonia," she said. "He has not left the house in a month. Training camp started, he didn't get picked up by another team, and he hasn't left the house since. He has not gone out once, not a single time, he's so embarrassed."

What??? Man, I had no idea, and never once did he let on like that's what was going on with him. I genuinely thought he was sick. Just as I was having my eyes opened to how brutal it can be to transition from the NFL back to regular life, my friend Nate Boyer, who we'll get to in a minute, was having THE EXACT SAME CONVERSATION, ten feet away. Only he was talking to one of his fellow former Green Beret brothers, about how the guy didn't feel safe leaving his house because he didn't feel like he fit in anywhere. He felt lost without his team, his crew, without his uniform. How was he supposed to be normal again?

Neither knew how to fit into "normal" society. Both felt they'd lost their team, their tribe. Both populations experience the same nightmare transitioning back into civilian life, and they're so deeply in the shit, they can't see it won't be that way forever . . . it can and will get better . . . with the right team in place again. Which is where MVP comes in. The commonality of veterans and athletes, and the inner shit they go through when the uniform comes off, is eerily similar. Obviously, I know the jobs are different, but the fuckedupness of losing that locker room, that structure, those bonds, and the loss of a shared goal, the loss of their tribe . . . it's equally brutal.

When vets come home, they actually, literally, get asked by people all the time in public, or at gatherings, "Oh, you are a combat vet? Wow, how many people did you kill?"

Dead serious. I was guilty of that too because it's so glorified in movies. We civilians see soldiers on TV, and in movies, smoking the bad guys, so to us it gets romanticized. Even more thoughtful representations of war, or military service, can't get anywhere near the real horror, bravery, and selflessness of these vets. But especially in the video game version of soldiering . . . there's so much shit we don't know. How fucked up is that?!?! You might not even believe it's something a human would say to a total stranger. But vets literally get bombarded with this question ALL THE TIME.

So, yeah, many of our vets dread this and don't want to risk dealing with this kind of bullshit every day of their lives. Can you blame 'em? You'd stay home too. (We have actually come up with an answer to that question for them to arm themselves with, but we'll get to that in a bit.)

Okay, so it's a little less intense for the athletes, but it still completely fucking sucks to be thought of as "you used to be (fill in name)." Or to have people come up to you and say, "Hey, you're not signed, well, have you called the Giants? What about the Cowboys?" *Oh, thank you so much for the awesome idea, dipshit. Why didn't my agent and I think to call those teams?!?! I'm sure, once I do, I'll have my career back, and everything will be dandy.*

Plus, when their careers are over, too often, the same restaurants that couldn't wait to show them off in the past now don't take their reservation. The lights and action are gone, which might be all right, except they're not the only things that are gone, so is their team, their support system. As an athlete, or a veteran, they were always told where to go, when to go, what to work on, what to study, who to eat with, when to eat, what time to be where, what their missions are, etc., etc. They lose their team, they lose their purpose, but also, they lose all structure.

One of our MVPers, Kami Craig, broke it down best. She is a total badass gangster, won two gold medals and a silver medal, representing the USA in water polo. Played her whole life. When she showed up to MVP, on her second session with us, she told us she felt like she went from being a child in kindergarten, where you're told where to eat, when to eat, who to sit with, when to go to your cubby. And then, *BAM*, you're dropped right into junior high. All of a sudden you've got your own locker, you're responsible for your own schedule, and you're like, "Where the fuck am I going here?" That's fucking scary. At least in school, you can ask someone where you're supposed to go. But that is difficult for many of us to do in the real world. So, yeah, the retired athletes, they stay home too. That scenario is easier to laugh off, sure, but it's still embarrassing. And it picks at the deeper wound, which is that they're feeling hopeless and lost.

Once I saw how similar their situations and challenges were, I figured let's put both groups together, so they can have a team to ask these questions of . . . a team to have their backs, and to give them a new sense of purpose. Combat vets look up to athletes, athletes look up to combat vets . . . I'm going to form a new team for them and give them a new uniform. And together, we are going to be that locker room again, that tribe, that support system both sorely have missed, in a way I didn't truly understand until now.

I'd gotten my first glimpse of this issue when I met Nate, back in 2014. That's when he strolled into Unbreakable and made a bee line right for me.

"I heard you're the guy to see if I want to play in the NFL," he said.

"Huh? Who are you?" I asked, sizing him up.

"I'm a senior at Texas, I'm their starting long-snapper, and I play safety."

"How are you a senior at Texas? You have fucking gray in your beard."

Ready for this one? Nate filled me in on what seemed to be a too-far-fetched-to-be-true story. He had been in the US Army Special Forces, a Green Beret no less, until he was thirty, and then, he'd used the Army's GI Bill to pay for his college education. He chose the University of Texas, because he knew they were a big military school. Well, even though he was a full decade older than most of the players, he'd walked onto the Texas football team.

Not just any football team. The Texas Longhorns, fresh off a national title and countless other years of barely matched success. They were a powerhouse. Yet, there was Mr. Gray in His Beard Sniper, trying to pull a Rudy (another great sports movie from the Longhorns' rival Notre Dame). Oh, and the difference is Rudy never had a sniper zeroed in on him for an hour in a gun fight in Iraq. Nate did.

Nate made the fucking football team. This is not a typo. His old ass walked on, tried out, and yes made the UT football team. Oh, but there's one more detail to throw in here . . . Nate never played high school football!! Simply put, Nate was just fucking different. This is beyond ludicrous. It's stupid. No Hollywood scriptwriter would even come up with such a stupid story because it could never, ever possibly be true. It's even too far-fetched for Hollywood. A hooker and billionaire business-man falling in love in Beverly Hills? Yup, no problem, but even that is less far-fetched than Nate's story . . . except it's true.

Oh, but it gets even more ridiculous. Turns out Nate was realllly fucking good at his other job of, ya know, chasing and killing terrorists. So, Admiral William H. McRaven, then the chancellor of the University of Texas system, as well as the head of Special Operations for the United States Armed Forces, put together a special team. Nate and about a dozen guys went overseas and worked with other Special Forces units to hunt the bad guys.

How about this arrangement? Nate would play football for the Longhorns, and the moment Nate's Texas team was done playing for the season, the military plucked him out, sent him overseas to chase terrorists, then, right before spring ball practice, he was plucked back out from the other side of the wire and returned to school to study and play football. He did this for three years. I shit you not, there is no exaggeration in these words.

Nate finished telling me all this, and he did the impossible . . . he left me speechless (maybe the most outlandish thing he ever did in all his accomplishments).

So of course I googled him, and sure enough, there was this crazy story of the thirty-year-old Green Beret who walked onto Texas's football team and still deployed for his country while attending the university.

I was floored.

Which was how he'd ended up a thirty-four-year-old veteran, asking me to train him up and break him into the NFL. Oh, and by the way, here's how he made Green Beret in the first place, during their workout, when all the other hopefuls were all dead from the workout, Nate did one mile of lunges, around the track, around all the other exhausted soldiers . . . the military realized, that day, this dude was different.

The next line I uttered changed Nate's life, little did I know at the time how much it would change mine: "I see what you've done, but I don't know what you CAN'T do, so, let's go walk this walk together." My exact quote to him.

I quickly built Nate a strategy. He trained at Unbreakable, and we bulked him up from 175 pounds to 240. He drank more protein shakes in that time period than any human I had ever seen. During that time I literally called every team in the NFL, being a complete, pushy pest because, well, persistence is key, and I have no boundaries and preached the motivating power/story of Nate Boyer. Two teams were interested, the Rams, which I had nothing to do with, and the Seahawks, for which I leaned on my relationship with their GM John Schneider and head coach Pete Carroll. Schneids got it right away, understood how cool of a story it was, how Nate's work ethic would hopefully trickle to everyone else . . . how he trained himself to never quit could permeate in that locker room. Hooked 'em! But before officially signing him, Pete Carroll called me and said, "Jay, what are you making us do?"

"Pete, THIS is the guy you want as your ninetieth guy, the shit the top half of the roster will learn from him . . . everyone will be better, suiting up every day next to this dude," I blared back.

"No, no, I get why we are signing him, but what if I have to cut him?" said Carroll.

"So? It's part of the game, just fucking cut him."

"Oh yeah, you say that now, but I'm not cutting this dude and then have him shoot me from a mile out!"

To which I responded "Not my problem, Pete!" and immediately hung up the phone on him.

So, yes, I helped Nate get signed to the Seattle Seahawks and helped him live out his lifelong dream of playing in the NFL. And then, yes, he got cut after one game. But did I mention the part where he got to live out his lifelong dream?!?!

Only problem was, now Nate was without a mission, so he was going to do what he'd always done . . . which was to get deployed overseas again and put his life on the line yet again.

No, dude, let's not do that!!! I love ya too much now to have you, ya know, get killed and shit.

Instead, I moved him into my house, hooked him up with my agents at William Morris, and started helping him to look around for something else to do. Fast forward to a few weeks later, when Nate and I were having our simultaneous phone calls.

Neither my football player friend nor Nate's veteran friend felt like they fit in anywhere. Logan's timeline comes in here, but I'm going to jump out of order and, well, I'm going to trust my ADD on this one and still hold off on how little Logan led to all this coming together.

I told you about my need to be of service and how it helps me battle my depression and the gray. So, I vowed to create a new team, just for them . . . for US.

This new team was "merging" vets with athletes (players), or MVP.

I know they didn't have the same job, but think about this: combat vets look up to pro athletes, pro athletes look up to combat vets, when you merge the two together . . . it turns out it's pretty fucking magical. Turns out, the vets took it to another level. They actually told our athletes, "You guys gave us a break from war. We would be out there on missions and, despite us fighting, we couldn't wait to get back to base to watch sports!"

So, we merged them together and took the coaching, training, and then life coaching we were already doing at Unbreakable and brought it to a vulnerable population that really needed some support, getting right between their ears, and for us all to heal together what's behind our rib cage.

But, in order to help them, we had to build it. So, in 2015, Nate went around to different LA-area homeless shelters, which are essentially barracks for vets with nowhere else to go. This was the beginning of a profound education for me, one that committed me to being of service in a bigger way. Just think about how fucked up the situation is for so many vets in this country.

Many guys and gals who go into the military, they're only seventeen or eighteen years old. Maybe they stay in for three, four, five . . . ten years. During that time, the pay sucks, so they have no savings. They've built up no credit. If they don't reenlist, they're basically told: "There's the door." A lot of them enlisted, in the first place, because they were running from something BAD at home . . . so, they're not going back there. Hell no!!! They have nowhere to go. And, yes, there is a Veterans Association, which is supposed to help with mental and physical health, job resources, community building. But let's just say when Nate drove around to shelters, he found PLENTY of guys, in the VA system, who were in need of extreme help, yesterday.

(Side note: Two years into our existence I had Sly Stallone, who was training at Unbreakable, come in and talk to the MVP group. His message? He made the classic movie *First Blood* almost forty years earlier, to shine light on some of the shit these veterans were going through after the uniform comes off. Yet here we were, forty years later, and our vets were still experiencing the same exact problems with life after the uniform comes off.)

And, holy shit, my athlete friends were also struggling in their post-career transitions, and a lot of them had a similar backstory. Think about it, what makes you driven enough to be at practice eight to twelve hours a day, for twenty years, to only compete for that Olympic gold once every four years? What makes you put on a football helmet, run down the field, and smash your head into refrigerator-sized dudes over and over and over again? What makes you take three steps up into a ring or cage, with the person across from you allowed to remove you from your consciousness? Something's fucking off about you going in.

I don't view this type of "off" as a detriment. I view it as uplifting. Off is a good thing!! That fuckedupness is beautiful. It's what makes us fucking different!! But being different doesn't feel good for vets or retired athletes, once they're on the outside. For the first time in years, they don't have a team. When you're an NFL player, or an Olympian, or a fighter, or a veteran, you've always had a team. You've always had something to focus on that made use of how different you were. Or at least distracted you from it.

One of the vets Nate brought into our first ever MVP session is a marine named Denver Morris. He was homeless. And he'd had three suicide attempts. He was from the 2/7 unit of the Marine Corps, which had been among the hardest hit during its deployments to Afghanistan and Iraq and the hardest hit by suicide. It's absolutely crushing. We started MVP at Unbreakable, with Denver bringing in eight other homeless vets. Plus, we had two retired football players. Two MMA fighters. Nate and me. That was our first huddle.

Now, here's where the universe really shows that it conspires to help us. Hear this loud and clear: THE UNIVERSE CONSPIRES TO HELP US! It is NOT against us! That was such a difficult idea for me to process. Having depression, I always thought my sky was falling, and everything was against me. As I type, I truly see how much the Universe has nudged me along, helped me, even when I loathed the lesson at the time. It has always conspired to help me . . . and you too, teammate.

But at MVP, we give the universe a hand, we lift each other as we climb. How do we go about it? It's actually so simple it's brilliant. We simply give them their locker room back. We give them their team again . . . and we open up to each other about our shit.

We start each MVP session with a half hour of intense exercise. The reason we do that is, it releases the right—what's the word I'm looking for . . . I've been hit in the head a lot, I fucking forget basic things sometimes . . . oh yeah—it releases the right ENDORPHINS in the brain.

But, also, I want them to have that feeling they've been missing since they played sports, since the military . . . of being able to look around and have their brother and their sister on their right and left again. To feel a part of something bigger than them, to know someone has their backs. And to be of service, by doing the same thing for their new teammates.

But also, some of the best, most raw, vulnerable talks I've ever had in my life came on a wrestling mat, or in a cage, after my teammates and I have beaten the dog shit out of each other. That is when we tend to open up the most, so I'm trying to re-create this in MVP.

I start off every session the same way, barking out: "Who's new here? Give me your name, sport, or branch of service, and any injuries that we have to deal with."

At our very first MVP, we had a guy say, "Oh, I can't work out."

"Why not?" I asked.

"Because of my right arm."

"Why?"

"Man, it fucking hurts. I have a bunch of shit wrong with it."

"You're in pain?" I asked.

"Yeah, man, it fucking sucks."

"Well, you're going to be in pain, whether you work out or not. You might as well work out with your team here and feel less shitty about yourself."

Pause . . . let him digest my words. He thought for a moment, couldn't really find an argument back then shrugged . . . he was in.

BAM! He was in.

It's that fucking simple! There's no big secret to why MVP works. It's just a matter of doing something many people have avoided for too long: showing up every week, facing the facts of how we feel, physically and emotionally, and choosing to push through it in order to be there for ourselves and for everyone else who showed up that day, probably also feeling shitty. Do that every week and, odds are, life will change.

We have amputees, champions, pro athletes of all kinds, people who have pulled themselves out of homelessness, world champion snipers, SEALs, people who are paralyzed, people who have world records . . . we all train TOGETHER. It's quite the sight.

We've got Kirstie Ennis, a Marine who is now an above-the-knee amputee after her helicopter went down in Afghanistan, and she's got her prosthetic on, and she's doing her kicks . . . just like everyone else, only adapted for her. Oh, a little more about Kirstie, despite enduring forty-six surgeries and four amputations of her leg, she has since gone on to summit Mount Kilimanjaro as well as several other top peaks in the world, she was the fifth-ranked Paralympic snowboarder in the world and has just finished her third master's degree. That's all. Ya, know, a normal Wednesday when you're fucking different.

We might have Kami, that badass Olympic water polo

champ. She's on the mat with a vet who is a badass sniper, but he got hit by a sniper himself. The bullet went through his spinal column, and now he's only able to move from the waist up. He's in his wheelchair, and she's on a physio ball, and they've both got their gloves on, and they're sparring. How cool is that?! Pretty fucking cool.

The training itself is only part of it. I make sure everyone is always clocking how amazing their team is, and how special they must be to also be a member: "Hey, dude, you worked out tonight with a fucking two-time Olympic gold medalist!!"

Meanwhile, I tell Kami: "Yo, Kami, you worked out tonight with a badass motherfucking Marine recon sniper!!"

I want them to take pride in their team and their place on it. I want them to brag about each other and brag about themselves. I don't mean brag in an arrogant way, but fuckin' ay, brag to show pride in yourself.

Let's be proud. I always try and find people's highlights and bring them out. Then, I try to teach them to do that for each other. Bragging up somebody else is fucking beautiful. We all need that in our lives. We need to be each other's hype-men and hype-women. And not just once or twice. We've got to do it over and over and over . . . until it sticks.

While the workout is bonding, the true magic of MVP is what I call our Huddle. We open up about shit the rest of the world would not truly understand . . . they wouldn't fit into OUR normal, at first that is, until I would get them to understand that vulnerability allows anybody to fit in together. While we do have a clinical therapist, sitting in each huddle, we all become each other's therapists, a bunch of badasses, empowering each other with peer-to-peer therapy.

Our main goal is to give everyone a safe place to be honest

about what's hurting them, what they're struggling with, and their successes too. But holy shit, the things we bring up in that huddle . . . way more jarring than the shit you see in movies. Most places, if you're dealing with this kind of intense trauma, and you're honest, they're going to fucking lock you up. In MVP, it's safe to say, "Fuck, I'm in so much fucking pain, I feel like fucking dying."

What you will ALWAYS hear back is, "Hey, we got you, we got your back, we're here for you."

And, always, always, always, we're working on flipping our MVPers' perspective. Now that we've been doing this long enough, the old guard helps the newbies when they come in, and WE ALL keep each other in line. It's a team effort. We lift as we climb. We learned that from one of our badass Army Rangers, bronze star recipient J. C. Glick.

Most of the times we don't want to fucking hear how we're so great. We want to feel shitty. It's easier to feel shitty, right? The pain of what we already know is bad, but it's a lot easier and less scary than the pain of going out of our comfort zone.

We drill them until they learn to speak with pride of what they've done, and where they're at now. There's no more of this kind of bullshit, like, "Oh man, I USED TO play in the NFL." Or "I USED TO be a Marine, but then I got blown up by an IUD, and now I'm fucked."

No, motherfucker, you played in the NFL!! That's something that 99.9999 percent of people could never, EVER do. Or you willingly fought in a cage or wrestled on a mat. That shit makes you different and, again, different is good. Different leads to success. Or you were an NHL or MLB athlete. Or you were a Navy SEAL. Or a platoon leader. Or a brave Marine who risked your life, and literally, in the case of many of our

MVPers, your limbs, for your brothers and sisters, and for your country, and came home with injuries on the outside . . . and on the inside.

Our central message for our MVP athletes is that it wasn't the uniform that made them great. It wasn't the team. Nope. Those were the payoffs. But it was what they have behind their rib cage that propelled them to beat out millions and millions and millions of others to play in the NFL, or to land on the Olympic team. That's who the fuck they are. That's who they are!! And that doesn't suddenly leave when the uniform comes off.

For our vets, it's the same thing, only even more intense. They do incredible fucking things overseas and truly have grace under fire, courage under pressure, they are loyal as shit to their teammates. They literally put their lives on the line. And then, they come back over here and are made to feel, *Ah, I'm different. I don't belong anywhere here.*

And I'm like, "No, motherfucker, you're different!! Different is good!!! Different leads to success." But who tells them this? Well, we do now!

I've seen people go through the worst shit . . . the suicides of their military brothers and sisters, addiction, relapses from sobriety, divorces, not getting custody of their kids, cancer, the death of family members . . . their MVP teammates are there for them. With text threads. And calls to check in and say hello, not just once, but every day, for as long as needed.

I've seen people give each other advice, support, pretty much anything and everything, including the shirt off their backs. If someone is really in the weeds, I might get a text from one of their MVP buddies, asking me to check in on them. When the MVPers I'm closest to can tell I'm in the weeds, they check in on me. That's the magic of this fucking circle. We don't need to have a fucking college degree from Harvard or Yale, or be a business leader, to do great things. This circle has a large number of formerly homeless people, a large number of people who have tried to kill themselves. People who earn minimum wage. It's the smartest group I've ever been around . . . Most powerful group, and we do it all, peer-to-peer, which means we do it TOGETHER.

Actually, it was the brilliance of our group that, in my opinion, may have given a solution to our vets for when people ask them that fucked-up question I brought up earlier: "How many people did you kill?"

Well, how about this? One of the things I literally had to force our vets to do was figure out something they were proud of during their service and say it aloud in our huddle. It was July 4 and I said, "Hey, this country was forged on you and alllll those before you, fighting for our freedom and the freedom of others around the world, so when those fireworks go off and we are all celebrating you, because that's what we are doing, what are YOU celebrating about yourself?"

Go ahead people. Do this at home right now. I NEED you to say something you are proud of. For our vets, it was amazing, they couldn't say it.

"Well, Jay, how are we supposed to be proud of killing people?" asked Denver.

"I didn't say that, Denver. I asked what are you PROUD of about your service. Doesn't have to be about killing someone."

"Man, this is hard, Jay," Nate said. "We are ingrained not to have individuality in the service. It's about the team not us individually."

"I hear you, Nate, but this is why so many of you struggle.

This is why the transition sucks so much. If you can't use your service in your next step in life, you're fucked. We need to start changing that NOW!"

They processed it . . . but they heard me eventually. Oh my goodness, the magic that poured out that July 4 and every one since! Tales of bravery, courage, protecting people, putting the first ever shoes on children in Afghanistan, being given gifts from brothers lost in battle, protecting the first ever democratic election in Iraq . . . on and on they went.

Then, a couple years into me asking this . . . more magic.

"Jay, I have always had a hard time talking about anything I am proud of in my time in the military," said one of our vets, Ben Effinger. "It's just not how we are wired. But you got to me in how you pushed us. So, after that huddle, I went home and for the first time I pulled my footlocker down and I showed some things to my eight-year-old son. I had a picture of a cache of roadside bombs we found before they could hit any of our troops. My son asked me about it and when I told him, he said, 'Wow, Dad, how many people do you think you . . .'

"'. . . saved?'"

And there, from an eight-year-old boy was the answer.

"There it is," I said to the group, puzzled by where I was going. "There is your answer, we just got it from your son, Ben. The next time someone asks you, 'How many people do you think you killed.' Ben's son just gave us the answer . . .

"I don't know but I saved a lot!"

The collective sigh of relief from the room, felt like the roar of a stadium. They all got it, they all needed it, they all found it . . . from an eight-year-old boy all because we decided to be proud. Look at how brilliant this group is! Look at how much we can learn from them. I do fully believe it is the wisdom from these huddles that can change the suicide rate and view of mental health in our world.

So why don't we take you even deeper inside our Huddle?

TEAMMATE, LET ME ASK YOU:

Who can you pass the message of the MVP way along to? Who do you know who's in need? Or who do you know who doesn't *seem* to be in need, but it couldn't hurt to tell them about it anyhow? Who do you want on your team? The time for connecting and building and being brutally fucking honest about what hurts us is now. People are literally dying every day. We all need to heal. I truly believe it's the lessons of this group that can help change the way we can attack the suicide rate in this country. Our veterans were so willing to open up and be vulnerable for this book . . . pass their lessons along! Honor them by passing their message along so they . . . and you . . . can be of service to others. The first step is to talk about everything. BECAUSE WE HAVE TO.

6

YOU NEVER KNOW WHAT
LIES AROUND NEXT TUESDAY,
THE LESSONS OF MVP

Picture this: eighty badass combat veterans and athletes, after having worked out together, are sitting in a circle on the wrestling mat next to the cage at Unbreakable Performance, the home and birthplace of MVP. Now, picture this: all eighty of us are crying. Men, women, big bad motherfucking NFL players, some of the most vicious cage fighters on the face of the Earth, men and women who've done incredible things for our country in battle, some of whom were literally the first ones in Afghanistan after 9/11. One of our vets, Danielle Baker, whose first day in the military actually happened to be 9/11, and just a few weeks later, she was the first one to put her boots on the ground in Afghanistan, as a chemical warfare specialist in a Special Operations group (yes, the badasses of badasses). I wanted to point this out, because she is just now learning from the Huddle how to brag about her badassery, so I never miss a chance to do it for her.

Again, eighty of the baddest mofos on the planet, and we are all openly sobbing.

"Fuckkkk man . . . fuck," says one of our veterans, his voice trembling. "One of my teammates I served with, we were supposed to get together Saturday. Friday, he calls me, but I'm swamped with work, and I figured I was going to see him the next day, so I didn't take his call."

He paused, trying to push his next sentence out.

"Well, I didn't see him Saturday because he killed himself that night. I didn't take his call! Why didn't I take his call?! What if I just took his call?"

I will let you all grab a breath as you absorb this, because it's a lot. Take a deep breath. Grab a tissue. It's okay. Ain't no shame in it.

THE FIRST THING I do at MVP, whenever we are faced with trauma, is throw the elephant in the room. Actually, every elephant. We talk about things as no-bullshit, raw and real as we can, because I want us to feel real. They are raw . . . so why wouldn't we talk about them that way? Push that elephant's big ass right into the middle of the room.

So, after our heartbroken vet had finished speaking, and we'd all been bulldozed by his words, I immediately repeated the first line I ever said in MVP . . . the very, very, first line in that first MVP session I wrote about in the last chapter. "Life is about our CHOICES, our DECISIONS . . . and our first choice is life or death, and you must decide to choose life! Not for yourself, but for everyone else. It's selfish as shit to take your own life and leave everyone else around you with more problems, more grief, more shit in our own fucked up lives. So, if you are going to do one thing right now . . . make the DECISION to CHOOSE life! Period, the end!"

Think of what that soldier did to his fellow veterans, and this teammate in particular. It's fucking awful, to leave him with this type of guilt. How does someone possibly get through that kind of remorse? So yeah, we need to attack it.

I am trying to villainize suicide, but at the same time, we are trying to lay out why this option was even on the table in the first place as a "solution" for those who were struggling. We need to examine the mindset and then beat it back with every tool we can. *Again, I know this sounds harsh, but I can only use the verbiage I have seen work in our group, and this is the language that has worked.*

We MUST make the DECISION to CHOOSE life! We need you here. We absolutely need you here, teammate. Every one of us, whether we see it or not, helps, lifts, empowers someone or many others over the course of our lives. You never know when that may be, but we need you around to do so. That's one major reason you need to choose life. But the other reason is the carnage you leave behind if you choose that other path. You will leave us in more pain, and often with major guilt about what we did wrong. We are the ones left asking, "What more could I have done?" Think about that for a minute. Finally, we also need you to choose life because when you choose suicide it opens the door for so many others to follow suit, others I'm sure you don't want to see suffer the same fate. I call this the "power of suggestion."

Let me clarify. Too often when a veteran commits suicide, I'm immediately alarmed that others will follow suit. It opens the door for others. And shit, with the prevalence of social media these days, the suggestion is even more readily available. When someone commits suicide, the outpouring of love and celebration of that person's life becomes incredibly grand. Think about it . . . other people who also have thought their lives suck, been distraught over their lack of what or where they want to be in life, and suddenly, they see such an outpouring of love. It makes them think, *Well, my life blows, I don't feel anyone appreciates me. I feel shitty, and I want people to cry for me. So, fuck, why wouldn't I take that route? Then I would finally feel loved and celebrated too.* That is what I mean by the power of suggestion. But we can't let that be a prevailing mindset. You can't go the suicide route. You just can't.

The battle against this power of suggestion is made even harder by social media. We live in a society where we are constantly comparing ourselves to someone else's "filtered" fraction of a second of their lives on Instagram, Facebook, Twitter, TikTok, so of course we often think our own lives suck. Or we feel left out of everyone else's "successes," many of which are full of shit, because they are filtered, edited, highlighted, or enhanced. So, yeah, of course, once again, we shit all over our own lives and what we've accomplished or where we are in our love lives, work lives, social lives, etc. Humans are not made to feel so left out. We also aren't ingrained to deal with so much hate and so many vicious comments. We just aren't.

So, yeah, I understand that this level of pain could cause many to look for a quick out. But that level of pain and guilt then gets passed on to us, the survivors. It's absolutely brutal.

Which brings us back to our MVP circle, with this veteran who was crying about what would have happened had he answered the phone for his teammate Friday night instead of just talking to him in person, as planned, on Saturday.

Then came my next statement, and this is the one I truly believe has saved more lives in our group than any other . . . the absolute game-changer of all the elephants I throw into the room:

"OK, look, many of us are crying in this Huddle right now. There's fucking eighty of us. Your friend who killed himself, whatever afterlife you believe in, do you think he's in it right now, looking at all of us, crying, hurting . . . do you think he's up there celebrating? Doing the happy dance to himself, yelling out, 'Yessss! Look at how I made all those fuckers cry! Yes! Yes! Yes!' Or do you think he's looking at all of us, saying, 'Nooooooo, what have I done? No, no, no! I didn't mean to do that to all my friends and family. Noooo, I wish I could take it all back and do it over again!'"

The room was tense. "Which one is more likely?" I continued.

I asked for a show of hands of how many people in the room either attempted suicide or have contemplated suicide in the past. Guess how many hands went up? Thirty? Forty? Fifty? How about damn near every single hand in the room. "Well, this is what you would have left behind!" I loudly implored. "But all of you now get to have a 'do over.' All of you. You get to see what you would have left behind, had you been successful in your past attempts. So, don't fucking try to leave us behind like that ever again!"

Can you imagine how many suicide victims would take a "do over" if they could have one? So, share this with others. Share it with anybody and everybody. "THIS is what you would have left behind!"

As the first five years passed in MVP, our MVPers continued to lose friends and men and women they'd served with, who weren't in MVP, to suicide. But our number stayed at "Fucking Zero."

One of our veterans came up with the slogan we adopted as our own: "Don't be one!"

Okay, just stay with me here, because I'm about to go on one of my ADD detours. But just bear with me. I was training a fighter, Ava Knight. She's a seven-time world champion in boxing, an absolute rock star as a human, and technically, the best boxer any of us at Unbreakable have ever seen. Literally, the best technical boxer, Couture, Liddell, or I have ever trained with in our lives. After a lengthy championship-filled boxing career, she started training with me in 2017 and I convinced her to move over to MMA for a bit. I wanted her to get a taste for the sport, which she liked, and to see if she could make the transition because I believed there would be a huge market for her. I often look for unconventional paths my friends and I can take to success, but I also needed to see how she would do incorporating wrestling, submissions, and kicks into her combat sports game. Her whole career was spent in a boxing ring and that fighting range was different.

The night before fights, we all still train. I don't know if the rest of the world knows this. You may think we all just rest. Nooooo, the night of weigh-ins, after we make weight, we then rehydrate before training again. Light training, but you need to get the fluid back in your muscles, or you'll just pee much of it out. Plus, we usually go over game plan and work on situations for the fight the next night.

Well, Ava, ummmm, how do I approach this? Ah, fuck it, why be shy now?

Ava said, "Coach, I got my period, and my stomach is killing me . . . what do I do?"

(Trust me, I'm going somewhere here, and it has to do with MVP, and how we kept our suicide rate at Fucking Zero for the first five years.)

I had nothing. She asked me, Randy Couture, Jay Hieron,

Jason Borba (our other coaches); collectively, we have trained over a thousand athletes and fighters. I looked at them, they looked at me . . . crickets. We had no answers. It wasn't a question a fighter had ever asked me before.

So I called my only other female fighter for advice on the spot. Demi Lovato. Yes, that was my "I'd like to phone a friend, Regis," call. (More on Demi and how she joined our fight team coming up.) I'm not name dropping here. But I've had Ava and Demi train a bunch together, and I knew Demi would have the answer, without me having to pussy-foot around.

I know, I know, you don't have any pop stars in your speed dial, but I'll bet there's someone you might be intimidated to reach out to for any number of reasons—because you think they're more successful, or more popular, or that they might be surprised to hear from you. Let me tell you, we all have those negative voices in our head (mine are just a little more vicious)—this whole book is about daring to connect anyhow. You never know, they probably need a teammate too. So, pick up the phone. Ask for advice. Ask for help. It will serve you both.

When I got Demi on the phone, she told me to get her a heating pad and some Midol. (Stay with me here, and yes, my life is not normal, but in my mind, calling one of the biggest pop stars in the world made sense to me, because Demi just talks real, and well, we consider her one of our fighters. Again, think about who your Demi is and don't be afraid to enlist their help.) I relayed what was not exactly ground-breaking advice to Ava, but because of the thirty minutes she needed to use the heating pad she was late coming downstairs into the hotel workout room. (Usually, a ballroom set up by the UFC, or Bellator, or whatever promotion you're fighting for.)

As I was waiting for her, there happened to be a *USA Today,* sitting on the table with a front-page headline that blared "Veteran suicides on the Rise." The article reported that despite all the attention now on veteran suicides, the rates in the past few years had increased dramatically; both the Army and Marines had double-digit increases. *Increases.*

Going back to what I said earlier, I was horrified by the power of suggestion, and how many would read this and then feel this was their "out" also.

I called my executive director of MVP and read him this story. Then, I asked, in all of our branches of MVP, in the four years we'd then been running MVP, how many of our active members have killed themselves.

"What is our total number?" I asked.

He paused for a moment.

Then, he said, "Jay, you won't believe this."

"What?" I asked. "How many?"

"We've had zero."

Huh? What? There's no way.

"Yeah, we've actually had zero."

"Fucking zero?"

"Yes, sir, fucking zero," he said.

Until that moment, until that article had appeared before me, I never knew, probably because I just hadn't asked.

Zero?!?! Wow.

Ava won her Bellator MMA debut the next night, via a vicious body-shot KO, but I also suddenly had a new thing to bring to the next MVP Huddle. I was so proud of coaching Ava to win her MMA debut, but she was prouder of the fact that we'd just learned of "Fucking Zero!"

Fast forward to Wednesday night and our next MVP Huddle. I replayed the entire story to the room—Demi, menstrual advice, and all—then asked the huddle the same question I'd asked. Did they know how many suicides we had had at that point in our group? There was a little light chatter among different members trying to figure out their answer before I loudly rejoiced with, "Fucking Zero!"

The emotional brilliance of this group comes shining through the strongest when we are at our most vulnerable.

"I need to say something," said former Army combat veteran John Follmer, the youngest person in his unit to actually enter a war zone in Iraq, which took place on his eighteenth birthday. "I feel I have to share this. Last week . . . I was going to kill myself." He just threw it right out there.

Wow, this room just took an unexpected turn.

"I committed to committing suicide," he went on. "I went into my gun safe, to do what I committed to, but somehow, my gun wasn't there. I looked on the other shelf in that safe. Gun wasn't there. I had no idea why my gun wasn't there, but in my mind, well, if you're going to dig a ditch and you don't have a shovel then you're not going to do that job of digging a ditch. Same thing here, I didn't have my tool, so I didn't do the job." Suddenly, Follmer started trembling. "Jay, and to the whole group . . . I am so sorry. I am so fucking sorry. I had no idea we haven't had a single member commit suicide. I am so sorry . . . I promise you . . . I won't be ONE."

Okay, breathe again. Just like earlier in this chapter, let the power of this sink in and take a quick breather as you're reading this. Let the wisdom and power of John Follmer's words sink in. From that day, we've had the saying "Don't be ONE!" Don't be the first member of our group to follow through with a suicide. Several of our MVPers have since told me they were seriously contemplating it. But then they heard me, or another member, barking "Don't be ONE" in their minds. And it steered them to hold on instead. Thank God Follmer didn't complete his attempt that day, because in the years since he has personally lifted up countless lives, done welfare checks on his brothers and sisters, and, quite frankly, he's been a blessing.

That was the first five years of MVP. Unfortunately, in 2020 during the pandemic, we lost one of our beloved members. It was hard for me to give up that "Don't be ONE" slogan, because I'd had vets tell me that slogan raced into their minds when they thought about taking their life. But I also know how brutal the daily battle is for our group, and I do honor all those who hang on for themselves and for us. I think if we can all get through the shit together, it allows us to speak more personally on the subject to others who also walk through the darkness.

I'm also proud of another slogan I blurted out in one of our earlier sessions that first year of MVP's existence: YOU NEVER KNOW WHAT LIES AROUND NEXT TUESDAY. As in, you'll never know when life will change for you. Some of the shittiest things that can ever happen, could, in fact, end up blessing the world. How many times have we felt despair from not getting a job or losing a relationship or having something completely shitty happen, only to one day have it all turn around? You just never know who you are going to meet that will change your life. You never know what will come into your life to suddenly empower you. You never know what lies around the corner . . . or next Tuesday, as I put it.

Okay, this FINALLY leads us back to little Logan. I know, I know, huge jump from when I first talked about him two chapters ago, but I really wasn't kidding about the whole ADD thing. As I mentioned earlier, I first met Logan Nobriga through the

previous charity I started called Touchdown Dreams. That organization helped so many great kids, all of whom had brutal
stories that could have crushed you . . . these cute, sweet, little
kids, facing off against the kind of gnarly shit that no one should
have to deal with. But out of all of those special kids, Logan and
I bonded. Like everyone else in the story of MVP, Logan is just
different.

He'd had it pretty rough. He'd had leukemia when he was
three. Beat it when he was six. And then, got sick again when
he was six and a half. He had to move back into UCLA Children's Hospital. I met him when he was seven, and he'd already
been enduring six months of chemo and radiation, plus being
cooped up away from all the fun stuff . . . and this was his
SECOND STINT. He'd been at UCLA Children's Hospital
for so long . . . more than half his childhood. Instead of getting
down about how unfair this was, he turned it around.

He kind of became the hospital's unofficial welcoming com-
mittee. When a new family was admitted, he took the kids
around and showed them where everything was and how it was
all done. At the same time, his mom, Kyrsha, became a guide for
the other parents. They were those kinds of people; even though
they were dealing with a mighty portion of suck, they were all
about giving back and helping others to lighten their own serving of suck. This little dude had it dialed in, and already, on his
own, he'd figured out the "Be of Service" part.

I just loved Logan and his positive attitude through the
chemo and the radiation. I saw him through some days when
the chemo was crushing him. I was also with him when a child
he became like a brother to in the hospital died. Logan had a
fighting spirit that I wanted to learn from.

As soon as he was well enough, I started taking him with me

everywhere—to football games, to the FOX studio. I started becoming closer with his family. Not just his mom, but also his grandmother, Suzi Landolphi, a licensed therapist who'd founded BIG Heart Ranch in Malibu, a ranch that helped combat veterans deal with the rigors after war, and those battling the temptation of suicide. Before that, Suzi worked at a retreat for combat veterans and first responders in Virginia, where they were providing therapy based on what they call post-traumatic growth.

It was his grandmother Suzi's connections that helped me launch MVP.

In November 2019, Logan turned fifteen. Thank God, he'd been in remission for four and a half years by this point. On his fifteenth birthday, I brought him to an MVP session at Unbreakable, and I had him look around.

Once again, we had upwards of eighty vets and players in the room.

"Logan, I know it fucking sucks that you had leukemia," I said. "I know it's terrible, but if you didn't, I wouldn't have met you. If I didn't meet you, we wouldn't have started MVP. I'm going to ask the room, if I didn't meet Logan, and we didn't start MVP . . . how many of you wouldn't be here right now?"

About thirty to forty hands went up. Almost forty people, right there in front of Logan, were admitting they would have taken their own lives if we hadn't started MVP.

"If we didn't have MVP how many of us wouldn't be doing as well as we are?" asked Thomas Harris, a Navy vet and one of the first ever members of MVP.

Every . . . single . . . hand . . . raised! This little guy helped us all in so many areas of our lives.

But then, something even more magical happened. It's

called gratitude. The gratitude that comes along with being of service. Hands started going up again, but this time it was for a different reason. Hands went up to talk to Logan. One by one, MVP members went around and introduced themselves.

"Logan, my name is Denver Morris. I did all these tours in Iraq and Afghanistan. I've lost twenty-one in Iraq, eight in Afghanistan. Since then, I've lost forty-five of my brothers to suicide. I've tried to commit suicide three times. If it wasn't for MVP, I would just be dead right now. So, thank you, Logan, thank you for saving my life."

Ummmm . . . tissue break.

"Logan, my name is Andi Ward, when I left the military, I had no self-worth, and I dealt with a lot of trauma," said one of our female vets. "I was hooked on drugs and alcohol, and I was homeless. This group changed my life. I'm now three years sober. I have a home, a job. I'm working toward my master's degree, and for the first time, I feel like I have a family who protects me. So, ummm, yeah, Logan, you saved my life too."

"Logan your leukemia was the catalyst for what we would learn to be MVP," said DiCarie Williamson, a twelve-year Air Force and Army Reserve veteran, who MVP inspired to pursue his doctorate in organizational change and leadership at USC. "We spend our lifetimes trying to figure out what our purpose is, and you received it at a very young age. The sickness you defeated (twice!) is the one thing that changed the trajectory of the lives of countless veterans and athletes. It reminds me of a quote by Steve Jobs where he said, 'We're here to make a dent in the universe . . .' and your victory over leukemia is just that. A huge dent in the universe. MVP is going to outlast all of us, and you, sir, delivered that gift."

"Logan, this is what you did, bro," I said.

"I didn't realize I did all this," he said.

Think about how powerful that is. Stories like these are why I always say, "You never know what lies around next Tuesday."

"Little bro, I don't know why you had leukemia, and I know it absolutely fucking SUCKEDDDD," I said to Logan, again, in front of the group. "But if you didn't have it, I wouldn't have met you, and if I didn't meet you, we wouldn't have MVP, and if we didn't have MVP . . . well, you see how many lives would have been lost."

Because of that suck, we have found so much beauty. You never know what lies around next Tuesday. So, thank you, Logan. Oh, and Logan . . . thank you for saving my life too.

Oh, and by the way . . . this was all just the magic of one huddle. We do this, together, every single week—we lift each other. Sometimes, we even save each other. Always, we learn from each other. And the lessons we teach each other in that circle are the lessons I am sharing with you now, so we can spread that magic, beyond our huddle, to the rest of the world. It is our way of being of service.

TEAMMATE, LET ME ASK YOU:

What was around next Tuesday for you? Think back to a time you got fired or dumped—or something much darker and shittier. Remember, you thought it was the end for you? But it ended up being the seed of something beautiful—the experience that connected you to your best friend, or gave you the empathy for the job you now have helping others, or cleared the deck for you to meet the love of your life. Or remember a door that closed that ended up changing your career, or life path, in a positive way. Look at it, let it sink in, embrace it, and thank the Universe for conspiring to help you when you didn't see it. Don't just keep this message to yourself either. Share it! BECAUSE YOU NEVER KNOW WHO NEEDS TO HEAR IT THE MOST.

THE PERILS OF BEING JAY GLAZER'S FRIEND (AKA USE LAUGHTER TO FIGHT THE GRAY)

Look, teammate, I know we just came off some heavy shit, talking about vets and suicide and homelessness, and all the crap some of our heroes go through, which is why I'm putting this chapter here. If ever there was a point where we need to laugh in this book, it's now. Well, I need to laugh often, and that's why I'm always doing whatever it takes to amuse myself. And I mean *always*, to the point where laughter has become the second pillar of how I fight the gray. I give you Exhibit A.

The Kansas City Chiefs had just finished up practice in training camp, back in 2008. One by one, they entered the locker room to peel off their uniforms and relieve their exhaustion from the previous two hours of hitting each other, again and again, in 100-degree weather. Each of the players sat down on their stools. But there, taped to the inside of each locker, was a Xeroxed copy of a porn video cover, starring none other than their captain and Pro Bowl tight end Tony Gonzalez. Only, Anthony Gonzalez was the name advertised in large, bold graphics across the top. Oh, but there was no mistaking the identity of the star of this skin flick.

The cover showed Tony Gonzalez, in full cop outfit with, well, his pants open. And these players AND his coaches had just been given the heads up about what Tony used to do for extra money . . . in his broke college years . . . or at least that's what his fucked-up NFL Insider friend was trying to get them to think.

And it worked . . . to perfection!

One by one, his teammates pulled the paper off their lockers, turned, and looked at Tony with a glance that screamed, "I fucking KNEW it!" Some actually used these exact words as they looked at Tony, and then back to what they were holding, then back to Tony.

Meanwhile, I was taking all this in, marveling at the power of my Photoshop skills.

Gonzalez spent the rest of the day explaining that it was fake, and that I, his friend, was an asshole. *Whoaaaaa, slow down there, sheriff. Lovable asshole is more like it.*

Yes, this episode is a by-product of being friends with a guy like me, who lives in the filth of gray. I need laughter to help me through, even if that laughter leaves casualties in the form of my friends. The good news is that the only possible collateral damage is to the pride of the person being pranked. And since we're all laughing together, and they're sometimes inspired to play along, I could even be helping some people around me who've been living in the gray without me knowing it. Right? Like how I'm turning this into a favor I'm doing for my friends? Oh, and it doesn't stop there.

Another time, Gonzalez—along with about two hundred other people in the NFL—received a text from me that read:

"Hey dude, some shit just went down, and your name came up, my phone is about to die, so call me at the hotel. I'm at this number 604-736- [whatever the last four digits were]."

I sent this to nearly every head coach in the NFL, over a hundred players, and several UFC fighters. Shit, I even sent it to my boss at FOX, George Greenberg (yeah, I'm THAT fucked up). I sent it to GMs around the league, team presidents. There was no position or status that offered protection from my fuckedupness.

When you get a text from a reporter with content of this nature, you obviously call back IMMEDIATELY. I counted on that likelihood for this particular prank.

Problem for them was, when my friends called the number, it wasn't to the hotel (I wasn't even staying at a hotel) but instead to a rather raunchy sex chat line . . . for $5.99 per minute!

One by one, the calls back to me started coming in:

"Hey dude . . . I called that number from a Pittsburgh Steelers phone! That shit is going to show up on the bill as being made from MY office phone!" exclaimed Mike Tomlin, the head coach of the famed and regal Pittsburgh Steelers.

"Hey asshole, I called right away and thought you were in a club, so I stayed on, yelling, 'Jayyyyy, Jayyyy,' thinking you couldn't hear me, until I realized what your ass did," said Jets then–head coach Rex Ryan. "So I didn't hang up right away and probably kept getting charged!"

Hmmmm, sure that's why you stayed on, Rex. Oh sureeeeeeee.

Beating the gray requires that I laugh *a lot*. You may be asking yourself right now, "If he's so depressed, why do I always see him laughing and smiling?"

Well, it's twofold: (1) to hide the pain behind my eyes, the pain I described in Chapter 3, of what it feels like to live in the gray, and (2) to use it as a defense mechanism (the second of my three pillars) to beat back the gray. My other tactics, such as "having a team" and "being of service," those are broader, more long-term solutions in combating the gray. But laughter is one of the few things that can dropkick me out of my darkest thoughts at any moment, right on the spot, any time I need a breath. It's an equally crucial survival mechanism in my arsenal due to its immediacy.

I can't tell you how many times I've been teetering on the edge of a really dark gray, fucked up wasteland of a valley, only to land the perfect prank on one of my boys and be pulled back from the brink. (I'd like to say the same goes for my friends, pulling pranks on me. But quite frankly, they aren't nearly as gifted as I am . . . I know, I know, I'm opening myself up for a fucking prank tsunami with a brazen statement like that, but it's the truth.) In twenty-eight years of friendship, I've gotten Strahan somewhere in the range of twenty to thirty times. He has gotten me . . . ummmm . . . TWICE. One of them was when the fucker dumped Gatorade on my head, during a live TV broadcast at FOX. Yes, the real story is . . . I actually never saw it coming. Bastard got me. (Every squirrel eventually finds a nut.)

Funny, people have said I have a Napoleon complex because of my height. I'm five-seven and an eighth and, oh yeah, you're damn right, I'm taking that one eighth, but that hasn't been it. Never was it. I don't have a Napoleon complex. I have a "depression complex." THIS is why I act out so much or try to be larger than life at times. It's not a lack of height. It's a lack of happiness. So, in order for me to cut through the gray and see some blue, yes, my friends have had to endure a lot. But shit, gang, think of the perks (I'm still reaching here). Laughter for me is literally an antidepressant/antianxiety/anti-gray pill, all wrapped up in one. That makes it dangerous to be my friend . . . or does it? You know why they deal with it? I hit it all the way back in Chapter 2, my loyalty. They keep coming back because they know I'm always there for them.

Strahan has talked about my loyalty, but he also talks just as much about my . . . immaturity. "You're selling your immaturity," he said one day at Unbreakable, right after I got done fucking with Sly Stallone, leaving the whole gym and Rocky laughing. "You're literally selling your immaturity."

Thank you for noticing, Stray.

I prefer to think of it like this: I bring a fun locker room to everyone. I bring a camaraderie, and yes, crudeness, and laugh-till-you-cry realness you can't find anywhere else. Anyone who's ever been on a team gets what I'm talking about. The measure of how much your teammates value you isn't how often they pass you the ball . . . but . . . how severely they fuck with you, and vice versa. And as we get more successful, we tend to become "Mr." or "Ms." to people, and others just get so damn serious around us. So instead, I bring that locker room, because we all need a team, no matter who, or how successful, we are. And we need to laugh . . . something I'm going to say many more times during this chapter, to really hit home how important this is, to beat the gray.

So, consider this chapter my greatest hits, if you will—an assortment of some of the funniest pranks I have played on some of the biggest names in my world. But before launching into them, I would like to take this moment to officially apologize (thank) all my friends who have long endured my jokes (fuckedupness) along the way. However, you all never even knew how much you were helping me out in the process. So, as you read this, I hope you take pride in acting as a gray-killer for me. (I'm really trying to weasel my way out of this shit, aren't I?)

Okay, here goes.

Let's start with Stray, especially since I told you about the time he got me. Since he's my best friend, you can imagine how much my "prank therapy" has landed on him. Whenever Strahan leaves his phone on the table to go to the bathroom, or whatever he's doing, I grab it and text someone something *realllllllly* fucked up from his phone, then erase the sent text, so he doesn't know he ever sent it.

One time, I texted his then-agent Maury Gostfrand (who is still my agent) from his phone, something totally ridiculous, about his bedroom fetishes.

Maury suddenly shot a text to Michael that read, "Are you serious?"

By now, Michael was back, reading his phone, and totally confused. "Am I serious about what?"

"What you just texted me?"

"Huh????"

"You just texted it to me!!"

"What the fuck are you talking about?"

(Meanwhile, I'm sitting across the table from Michael, perfecting my most innocent/angelic smile.)

Ahhhh, ain't no gray in these woods right now.

This is one of my signature moves, and I really could care less if I know the person or not. I pulled these texts off on my friends for years until, eventually, they all got wise to me and set up a lock function on their phones; so I had to find new unsuspecting targets. One day I was at lunch in San Francisco with Michael; our friend, an NFL agent named Doug Hendrickson; and his friend, Gavin Newsom. Yes, THAT Gavin Newsom.

Governor of California Gavin Newsom. This was the first time we had ever met, and Strahan had somehow managed to bring the conversation around to a warning against falling prey to my text-capades. Oh, I remember now. Michael brought it up because I had gotten him earlier that day, when I texted his girlfriend, from his phone, a rather embarrassing prognosis he had received from his doctor that he had previously been too embarrassed to reveal to her.

Unfortunately, the text back from her read, "Hi Jay."

Damn! Foiled again.

So, yes, the burn was fresh in his mind, and he told Newsom and Hendrickson what I had done. And yet, despite laughing at the story just minutes before, sure enough, Newsom turned to talk to the people at the next table and left his phone right there in front of me. His fault, right? I started to reach over for it. Michael's eyes widened. "NO!" he said quietly, under his breath.

"Shut up," I whispered back.

He started to say something else, but I was locked and loaded on my target.

"Shut it," I said again.

I sneakily grabbed Gavin's phone, looked down on the screen and . . . jackpot. His last text was from former president of the United States Bill Clinton. So, I was getting ready to text Bill Clinton something really fucked up, about a blue dress, or something like that when Gavin turned back around. "Nnnnnnnoooooooo," he blurted out. He jumped over the table, grabbed his phone back from me, and with eyes wide open, looked at me in something of a state of shock.

"Were you really going to text Bill Clinton from my phone?"

"Absolutely."

He looked disbelievingly at Michael, who said, "I told you, Gavin, he's fucked up. I tried to tell you."

NO ONE is off limits. Why? Because depression hates laughter, in any form, so it's necessary that I make myself laugh in any situation, even for a few seconds, to give my soul a break.

Another of my all-time favorites also included Strahan (poor bastard). I've got one more with him, then we'll give him a break and let him recover. One night, we had dinner at Merchants, a restaurant on the Upper East Side of Manhattan. Our waiter there was just a total dick from the moment we were seated and acted as if he was too good to even talk to us, because in his mind he wasn't a waiter; he was "an artiste." (I believe these were the words he used.) *Well, can you then "act" like a good waiter?*

Let me tell you, I've been around plenty of actors and artists who started as waiters. In fact, you're talking to one right here, I waitered, bar backed, bartended, bounced. You name it I did it, to make ends meet. I did this for five years in the early days when I was trying to find a job in sports. Even though I was trying to be a sportscaster, I still was a fucking waiter, or bar back, or whatever it was, when I was on that job. I made a million daiquiris to pay my rent. I can relate to a tough day on the job. But holy fuck, this dude was TERRIBLE to us.

So, when he dropped our bill at the end of our meal, I decided to make a point. I pulled out my Blue Cross Blue Shield health insurance card, because it looks like a credit card, and put it down with the bill.

Michael watched all this, shaking his head, knowing just how far I'd take it. "Stop."

"No, fuck this dude, he's been such an asshole to us." Might as well use his asshole-ness to pull my ass out of the gray a little.

So, the guy went over to the restaurant's computer system

and tried running the card. This kind of stuff makes Michael so uncomfortable, which, let's be honest, is most of the fun. He was halfway out of his chair, wanting to get the fuck out of there before the waiter returned. Too late. "I know I'm wearing all white, but I'm not a doctor," the waiter said.

I completely deadpanned my response: "I don't get it." Zero smile, faking total confusion on my end.

"You gave me a health card, an insurance card."

"Yeah, I know, I'm covered here."

"Oh no," Michael said, groaning.

"You're . . . covered here?" the waiter asked, legitimately perplexed.

"Listen, man, I'm not going through this again. I met my deductible earlier in the year. This is one of the restaurants in my network coverage. I'm not going through this again. Seriously, it's just too much. Run it again. This is why I paid for premium coverage."

He hesitated. Obviously, there was no way this could be true. But I was so convincing in my performance that he finally went back . . . and tried to run the card again! *Who does that?*

By now, Michael was essentially hiding under the table. "Can we please fucking leave? Please, PLEASE!"

"Oh, no chance," I said. "We are seeing this through." (Did I mention that I'm stubborn too?)

Finally, the waiter's manager approached him, and the waiter showed him my card. His manager looked at the card and then back at him. "It's a freaking health insurance card!"

The waiter, even more confused, but now defeated, returned to our table, card extended. "I'm sorry but this is a . . ."

"Hey, hey, I know it is," I said. "I was just fucking with you because you were such a dick to us. I figured you can't really be

THIS much of a stuck-up dick, so you must be having a bad day. Thought you could use a laugh."

"Was I really?" he said.

"Complete asshole to us."

"Really? I'm so sorry, and yes, actually, I've had a bad day."

"Well, hope this can give you a little laugh to help you out a little."

He started to laugh. "Actually, it did," he said. "It's okay. Thank you for that."

Yup, Mr. Artiste actually thanked me.

"Michael, you good?" I asked, finally giving the waiter my credit card to pay.

"No, I'm scarred," Michael said, shaking his head. "Only you can do something so ridiculously stupid and then be friends with the guy after."

Strahan *loves* to tell people that story. He's even told it on, I think, *Good Morning America*, or one of the nineteen other TV shows he's on. Because it's fucking funny. And it created a moment of connection with that waiter, who was stuck in his own shitty little world of gray. Laughter helped him snap out of it.

Oh, and here's a side note . . . about being raw and real with people. It's not always easy for them to handle in the moment. But that's partly because it's so rare. More often, when people are having a bad day, they're met with conflict or avoidance. The person across from them either escalates the situation or ignores that they're obviously struggling. It takes more vulnerability and presence to actually acknowledge where they're at, and to get in there with them, maybe try to lighten the mood, but definitely just let them know someone else sees them and what they're going through. If we could all start doing this a little more often, think how much better it would be for our mental health. Sometimes people would check in on us—and sometimes we'd check in on them—and it would go back and forth, and everyone would always have some support. It's sort of like building a mini-team, right there in the moment . . . even if the connection is temporary, it can really help.

Plus, the people in your life KNOW you are always going to be you, and you are always going to treat them the same, no matter how successful they become . . . or how many other people kiss their ass all day long. That's friendship. That's being authentic, another important principle I'll get to in a bit.

As much as I've pranked Strahan over the years, he hasn't even been my main target. I have saved that guy for last. Oh yeah, my muse. It will probably surprise you, but the man I have targeted the most with my pranks over the last twenty years is none other than Howie Long. Yeah, the Howie Long who had a thirteen-year career as a defensive end for the Raiders, Pro Bowl eight times, three first-team All-Pro selections, Super Bowl champion, and, the elite of the elite, inducted into the Pro Football Hall of Fame in 2000. He's been an actor and studio analyst for FOX since '94, and even had a show, *Howie Long's Tough Guys*, where he gave trucks to the NFL players that he decided were the toughest. Oh yeah, and he's six-five and still built like a monster. In fact, he looks like he should have bolts coming out of his neck. The same Howie Long that walked into the 49ers locker room after a game, looking to beat the fuck out of their offensive line coach and had none of the 49ers nut up enough to stop him. Can you imagine that? An enraged Number 75 walked into an opposing team's locker room, ready to take on the entire place because he felt offensive line coach Bob McKittrick had coached the Niners' lineman to target his knees, and the knees of his teammates. Ronnie Lott finally reasoned with Howie and calmed him down enough to get him to head back to his own locker room.

Yes, THIS scary SOB is my primary target . . . exactly the type of guys I like fucking with because everybody else is afraid to.

First, let me say that Howie is so incredibly special and important to me. He was someone I leaned on to learn how to be a good dad. I met my son, Sammy, when he was two and adopted him after his mom and I divorced a few years later. The way I figured, it wasn't his fault his mom and I split, and he already knew me as "Daddy." So, I adopted him, because I felt it was the right thing to do, but more importantly, because I love him and love telling him every single day of his life that I love him. That's why!

However, his mom and I split custody, fifty/fifty, and at the time, as a single dad, shit . . . I became an Instant Dad and had no idea what I was doing. So I watched and learned from Howie. We spent so many days talking about fatherhood in the most beautiful way. So you'd think this would buy him protection from me, right?

Even his own family relishes it when I fuck with him because, as his son Kyle says, "Nobody else will!"

My favorite joke I've ever hit him with, well, picture this . . .

Howie came to my house to visit me after ankle surgery, and while he was talking to one of my other guests, I snuck out, crutches and all, and put a rather large and obnoxious bumper sticker on Howie's truck.

Serious, intense, badass Howie Long, driving around Beverly Hills with a bumper sticker on his truck that read, in very large block letters, "I Love Porn."

Who the fuck would do that? This guy right here, that's who.

The next morning, at our FOX NFL Sunday production meeting, Howie loudly interrupted the start of the meeting, "Oh, by the way, let me tell you what your boy did yesterday." And he pointed at me. "Here I am, being a good friend, visiting him after his surgery, and somehow, the little fucker gets outside and puts this bumper sticker on my car. I'm driving around Beverly Hills for about fifteen minutes, and people are pulling up next to me, honking, some are giving me a huge thumbs-up. Man, I was so confused . . . and then I found out why! I pulled into my hotel, and there it is, for everyone to see . . . Yup, 'I Love Porn'!"

The room exploded; Bradshaw damn near fell out of his seat. Strahan and Curt buckled over. Jimmy Johnson, who was sitting next to me, got all red and asked, "Did you really? Did you really?"

Oh, ya, damn right, Coach.

I spoke up, defending my actions. Of course, I did. "Hey, in all fairness to me, I don't know for a fact that you don't love porn, soooooooooo . . ."

Two months later, I got him with another bumper sticker, the content of which I'll leave to your imagination because it's even worse than the first one. Shortly after he realized he had driven around town for thirty minutes with yet another doozy on his truck, I received a phone call from a screaming Mr. Long.

"Did you put another bumper sticker on my car?!?!"

"Ummm, who is this? Mom?"

"Hey, asshole, did you put another bumper sticker on my car?" he asked, now wanting to kill me.

"Well, um, hmm, I'm not quite sure, I don't remember . . . I might have, but I can't remember."

"YOU CAN'T REMEMBER?!?! What do you mean you can't remember?!?!"

I guess he had a point. It was a particularly raunchy and very memorable slogan I'd chosen *just* for him—so my clueless act was only winding him up more.

Okay, one more with Howie. I used to get his flight information from our assistant, and one time, when he was flying out after the show, I timed it to where I knew he would be sitting in his plane seat. I sent him a text, one in which you can't turn the sound off when you open it to read.

He opened it and there, playing loud and proud on his screen, was a graphic video of a very untalented stripper, jumping off a stage onto customers' faces, with the screams accompanying it. And there was Mr. Serious, not able to turn it off. Turns out, he was sitting next to an elderly lady on that flight.

To that I say, "You're welcome, ma'am."

"Jay, what if I die and that's the last thing that's on my phone, what are people going to think?" he loudly asked me later.

"Gee, that's a great question. Yes, what *are* they going to think?" I responded.

There was also that time I gave Howie a fake scratch-off instant lottery ticket that "won him" $25,000. Shit, before that I had Daniel Cormier, former UFC Light Heavyweight Champion of the World, give one of these very tickets to his friend, then–Penn State wrestler David Taylor, who'd just been crowned NCAA national champion. Taylor immediately flipped out when he thought he'd won $25,000. I told Cormier, "He's your friend, you get to be the one to tell him." It was as if the poor bastard had just lost twenty-five grand.

Hey, this is the price of being friends with Jay Glazer.

It's not just players who get it. Coaches are in my crosshairs too. One coach I love to prank is former head coach of the Panthers, Broncos, and Bears, John Fox, who everyone in the NFL calls Foxie. One night we were at dinner at Shanahan's Steak-house in Denver, owned by Mike Shanahan, the former head coach of the Broncos. After dinner, the waitress brought the check, and Foxie grabbed it and immediately paid. When the waitress brought the bill back for him to sign, Foxie had forgotten his glasses. So I told him I would fill it in for him and sign, since he couldn't see shit.

However, instead of what normal people do—because what are normal people and what the fuck is normal?—I left a *negative* tip amount and then, yes, subtracted it from the bill. The bill was around $250, but I put down a minus-150 and then totaled it to be $100. And then, I signed it.

Poor gal. She came over, holding the bill, studying it in confusion. "Excuse me, Coach Fox. Was there a problem with the service?"

To which I chimed in to the waitress, before quickly walking away to leave him with the mess, "I thought the service was impeccable, not sure what his issue was."

Exit stage left as I quickly slipped away.

"Huh, what do you mean?" he asked.

"Well, you left me a negative tip," she said, holding it out to him.

I was waiting outside at valet when he finished up. He walked outside and barked, "Hey, dickhead, you left her a negative tip . . . under my name??? Who the fuck would think of that?"

Great question. Who *would*?

Look, I know that the jokes I play on these cats make me a target for revenge, but that's a risk I'm willing to take. Because whether I dish it out, or I'm someday the recipient, each bout of laughter takes me one step closer to seeing streaks of blue. Sure, my pranks are juvenile and sometimes a little crude. I won't fight you on that. But here's the other thing I've found to be true over the years: we live in a world where most people are trying to fit in, to seem cool, and to pass for normal, even if it means hiding who they really are or what would actually make them happy. So, when someone comes along who is just totally unabashedly fucking ridiculous, it makes a BIG impression. It's like a breath of freedom! Not just for those of you who struggle, but for anyone out there, because not every day is filled with rainbows and unicorns.

Even just the threat of a joke sometimes lifts us up in ways we could never expect. It actually helped me get onto *Ballers*. I get these questions all the time, "How did you get on *Ballers*?" "How long were you an actor before you got cast?" An actor??? Shitttt, I'm no actor, I'm just an asshole with equally asshole-ish friends. So, here is the honest truth.

On my second day, I was set to film a scene with Dwayne in the gym. When I arrived, the production team sent me to the makeup trailer. I didn't understand. I was just training with The Rock . . . what did I need makeup for?

"You are not just training," the makeup artists told me, while I sat in the makeup chair. "You have a lot of dialogue. You have like thirty lines."

"No, I don't."

We went back and forth on this point several times, and then I finally got it . . . OH! Okay, The Rock is going to get me. He's trying to set my ass up. Well, I'm not fucking falling for it.

When I got to set, the director came over. It wasn't the same director we'd had the day before. For *Fox NFL Sunday*, we have one producer and one director, and they are a constant team. It seemed crazy that, all of a the sudden, in the SAME episode, we had one director for one day, and another director for the next one.

This guy was British. I took one look at him, and I could see right through him. This guy's clearly an actor they brought in to play the director, just to fuck with me. Nope, I'm not going to be THAT guy who starts flipping out when they get me, because I don't know my script. No shot.

"Okay, Jay, do you want me to run your lines with you?" he asked me.

"Nah, I'm good," I said, oh so smugly. The whole time, I was looking at the cameras pointed at me and thinking, *I'm getting punked. They're trying to get me to shit my pants that I don't know my lines. There's no fucking way I'm going to let this happen.* Despite my protests, the British director started running lines . . . *Wow, he is saying A LOT of fucking lines. Man, they've really gone overboard on this elaborate trick they're playing on me.*

"Jay . . . do you know your lines?" the director asked again.

"I'm good, don't you worry, I got it," I said, even more smugly, because I felt he was mic'd up.

"You need to learn your lines. We have five minutes before Dwayne comes out."

I wasn't budging. You can't "Glaze" me . . . that was until The Rock's stand-in came over and asked me if I wanted to run lines.

"I know what you motherfuckers are doing," I said.

"Mr. Glazer, I'm Dwayne's stand-in," the guy said. "I'm not sure what you're thinking, exactly, but I'm telling you, you've got like thirty lines, man. I promise you."

"You're not fucking with me?"

"Jay, I promise you, I wouldn't do that to you. I promise."

Fuck. I now had two minutes to learn thirty lines. *Fuckkkkkkk!* The lesson here? The best way to get me is let me get myself. I should have known The Rock wasn't *that* good.

Luckily, the lines I added, because I didn't have enough time to learn my ACTUAL lines, ended up being hilarious, and we used them on the episode. As I told them all afterward, I was "playing my normal dickhead self, and I'm reallllly good at playing that!" So, after my first impromptu, on-set rewrite went so well, they gave me a little more leeway. That became a recurring theme during my five seasons there. Eventually it got to the point where I was told there were scripts. And then, there were what one of the producers said they called "Glazer scripts," which was this shit they knew I just wasn't going to follow anyway.

But what REALLY made the crew—and viewers at home—snort their drinks out their noses, was me just fucking with Dwayne. He may seem like he's so perfect. Hell, he *is* pretty perfect. But he is still a fucking dude, a dudely dude, who played football, and wrestled, and lived in that super machismo world. But now, as he's become the most famous man on the planet, he's lost those old locker rooms of football and wrestling. Everyone, yes, even including The Rock, needs his team.

The best pranks are played on those who are on your team, in your circle—that's what makes the laughs so big, and what causes those laughs to grow the friendship/bond you've built.

All this is the perfect lead up to my third pillar of beating the gray . . . and it falls right in line with what I was just talking about

HAVE A TEAM, not just for the jokes, but rather, for a much bigger purpose.

TEAMMATE, LET ME ASK YOU:

How can you do a little "prank therapy" in your own life? Are you the one who needs to laugh? (Who fucking doesn't?) Which of your teammates are most likely to put a smile on your face, either because of their humor, or because they're so gullible, they're the perfect target for your fucked-up genius? All's fair in fighting the gray! Or who do you know who really needs a laugh? What can you do to give it to them? Whatever it takes today, either with someone or alone, laugh. Oh, and rule of thumb, MAKE IT HARMLESS! The strategy here is to laugh, because that breaks up the gray, but let's not have our jokes make someone else feel shitty. I have one friend in this book who shall remain nameless (ah, fuck it, it's Chuck Liddell) who hired a Mexican Federale officer to "arrest" his friend while on vacation. All while Chuck was laughing his ass off in the next room, as this poor bastard saw his life flash before his eyes. So, the moral of the story is, ummm, don't do that. The key to a joke or getting a laugh . . . all parties benefit. You all get to enjoy the beautiful power of laughter . . . BECAUSE THE GRAY HATES LAUGHTER.

8

FIND YOUR TEAM

Demi Lovato snatched her handbag, turned to the rest of us inside my gym, Unbreakable Performance Center, and boomed, "Nobody fuckin' follow me!" Out the door she went.

Yes, that Demi Lovato, one of the biggest pop stars in the world, the one with the Grammy-esque voice and the even bigger social media following. Demi is different. She can sing like very few in the history of this world, but she's also different like I am different, like many others who are reading this are different, which is why she was brought to me at Unbreakable in the first place.

Since, as she has talked about in numerous interviews, she has an addictive personality, her management team figured we could get her addicted to fighting, literally and figuratively. (Oh, and by the way, that little fucker can fight! She hits hard, and her kicks and elbow strikes are vicious. She even knocked out my front tooth last year when she threw a spinning elbow at me . . .

that I had taught her! We were lightly moving around, operative word here being *lightly*, when suddenly, *crack*, right through my mouthpiece went her elbow. My whole crown popped out. Millions saw my missing tooth, because she posted it on Instagram, but nobody knew what actually happened to thwack it out in the moments before. Yup, spinning elbow. Geesh.)

Anyways, back to why she came to Unbreakable in the first place. The idea was to replace drugs with boxing, alcohol with Muy Thai, her eating disorder with jiu-jitsu, and to give her a "fight team" to tackle what goes on between her ears and behind her eyes, alongside others who are like her and who truly get her.

But this was her first day of training and, especially at our gym, it's easy to look bad at first, because it's new and anything new is often hard. Why? The fear of the unknown makes us all stress. Plus, most everyone hates not being good at something right away, even though there's no reason to feel this way. Inside Unbreakable, our people really need to grasp the art of checking our egos at the door. We give the gift of "failing." Damn right it's a gift. Adversity is the best present we could ever give someone.

But Demi wasn't having that, so she got up off the mat in the middle of a drill, barked at my coaches again, "Nobody fuckin' follow me," and bolted. A half hour passed, and her team located her down the street and brought her back to Unbreakable. When she walked back in, she came right over to me and . . . fell into my chest, crying. "I'm so sorry, I'm so sorry, I am just in so much pain, I'm sorry."

God I loved how raw this girl was. I viewed her as brave and beautiful for showing me her flaws and pain. Her vulnerability was even bigger than her voice.

My response jolted her and changed the course of our history and our relationship forever. "Hey, I know you feel like you're fucked up, but every one of us who walk into that cage over there," I said pointing to the mixed martial arts cage that makes up a big piece of the Unbreakable soul. "Every one of us who walks in there, we are all fucked up, but Demi, we are good with our fuckedupness!

"What that cage does for us is it gives us a fight team, inside and outside of these walls," I continued. "You know what a team does? When the roommates in your head are starting to talk shit too loud, and the gray is getting bad, when you have a team . . . it gets those roommates to talk a little nicer to each other, and that gray to start to part. Your team can lift you up." (This is where things get real.) "But if your little ass runs out of here, and you run out on your team, well, not only can we not lift you up but . . . HOW THE FUCK ARE YOU GOING TO LIFT US UP?!" I shouted that line with heart . . . and heat.

Silence. She just looked at me. I didn't know if she was about to tell me to fuck off, for talking to her that way, or start crying again and run back out.

Instead? Her eyes widened and . . . "I get it," she said.

"You do?" I asked, shocked.

"I get it, I completely get it."

"You get it?"

"I get it."

"Okay, well don't be late next time either!" Shit, I had to take my shot when I could, laughing on the inside as I said it. (And look at it this way, if I could coach one of the biggest pop stars in the world with this kind of rawness and demand for accountability, just think how you can use these tools to reach someone in your life who's struggling.)

She got it. She stayed true to her word. For the next several years, and to this day, Demi and I have had our fight team to rely on. When Demi's shit got bad, we would often open Unbreakable, and the cage and all it represented, for her at all hours of the night, so we could have a "cage talk." The kind of talks that only we would understand, when the gray was getting really bad and the roommates in our heads were talking all sorts of dangerous, painful shit. Having a good team is a twenty-four/seven proposition. It has no off-days or downtime.

Her pain was evident when she nearly lost her life to her widely reported heroin and fentanyl OD in July 2018. We were at Unbreakable, waiting for her to come train, when we got the call. You know what we did? We rallied around her. We didn't shame her. We were there for her the whole way. Even when she was in rehab and recovery, she would call me to . . . *check on me.* THAT is what a team does.

As she has been quite public about, Demi was diagnosed with bipolar. I suffer from depression and anxiety. Some of us have depression that ensues in a lifelong battle. Some go up and down between the gray and the blue. Some who live in the blue may live with others who go through the gray. That's why the third pillar you can use to fight back against the gray is to "have a team," or in my case, to have "teams." I need several because my gray is so aggressive in its attempts to keep me in its darker waters.

Just like I told Demi, when you have a team around you, the roommates in your head start talking way, way, way nicer to each other, and some streaks of blue even come bursting through.

So, go find your team or teams. There can be a variety of teams in our lives. We just can't go at this world by ourselves.

You've already got me on your team. Now, find others like you, who resonate with you . . . it could be others who enjoy the same passions or hobbies, have the same job as you, or share the same faith. If there's one good thing about life in the time of social media, it's that it's easier than ever to find groups of people who are into the same things as you.

I'm not just talking about finding other people who like to golf or bike, or other uplifting pastimes like that, although, sure if that's what you're into, build those teams too. But also, others who share the same struggles or traumas with you. One trait I look for in my potential teammates is others who are kind of fucked up, like me. People who are different. My teams are different.

Not only am I trying to smash the stigma that being different is bad, I'm trying to glorify it these days. I've even made it be one of our MVP tentpole sayings: #MotherfuckerI'mDifferent. Yup, foul language and all, because the gray isn't sophisticated and all high and mighty; it's dirty and disgusting. I speak to it the way it should be spoken to.

I started Unbreakable partly as a business and partly as a mental health facility for my issues and for others like me. The physical part of my training helps my mental part, but even more than achieving physical strength, the real goal has been to build a place that would help me and others to cut through the gray more. I built Unbreakable around the fact that the world is a scary place to navigate these days mentally and emotionally. It has grown way beyond the four walls of the gym and the hearts of the people who train there, and we're taking new members every day. So, come be part of our new team, and the world will be much less scary pavement to roam. We will all walk this walk together, teammate.

By the way, the reason I need several teams is to help defend me on several different fronts. One day my *FOX NFL Sunday* team may be what lifts me up. Another day my Unbreakable team is just what the doctor ordered. One team can help create another. That's how MVP went from an idea to a mission. I didn't tell you this part earlier, when I wrote of the MVP way, but the very first conversation I had with a retired combat veteran, who was clearly struggling, happened right outside our doors at Unbreakable. Little did either of us know that this one conversation would turn into another one of the tentpole sayings of our whole MVP movement.

Meet Elliot Ruiz, one of the youngest Marines to ever deploy to Iraq as part of the 1st Marine Division, the biggest (and oldest) active-duty division of the US Marine Corps. Sounds pretty badass, right? Except when Ruiz first came into Unbreakable, his eyes were always downcast. He had an obvious limp, so it was clear he'd been through some serious shit. But it was more than just physical. He couldn't stand to make eye contact; his whole vibe was doom and gloom. He seemed, just . . . broken.

Well, you know me by now. I'm not gonna pretend something isn't happening when it's right in front of me. That first time I met Elliot, I looked him in the eyes and very bluntly asked: "What's up with you? Why do you always come in here all doom and gloom?"

"Ah, man, I got injured in Iraq, and now my wife has to put my pants on for me. I've had fourteen surgeries. Man, it's tough."

"Oh, man, sorry to hear that. Why have you had so many surgeries? What happened?"

"Well, I was on this one mission where my unit saved these

seven American POWs. I helped set up the perimeter, and then, once we got one of them out, the Taliban or whoever it was tried to get them back. Well, I had to shoot up this truck that ran the checkpoint. The truck flipped over, hit the razor wire, and the razor wire grabbed my leg and took me for a ride about a hundred fifty yards. I've got major leg damage, and actually it caused me to have multiple sclerosis, so, yeah, man, that's why my wife has to help me put on my pants."

OK . . . mouth . . . officially . . . on . . . floor. I was floored by his pain, but even more so, floored by his bravery. I needed to help him shift his perspective *IMMEDIATELY.*

"Hold on, hold on, back the fuck up! Did you just say you saved American POWs?"

"Yeah, but . . ."

"No, no, no, no, no. Stop with the 'Yeah, but.' There is no 'Yeah, but.' You just said you saved American POWs!?!"

"Yeah?"

"You SAVED American POWs? I just want to make sure I got this right."

"Ummmm, yeah, but the razor wire . . ."

"Stop, dude. Are you fucking kidding me? You saved American POWs? I've been around a lot of people who have done a lot of amazing shit, but I've never met anyone who saved American POWs. Here is what I want you to do: from now on, when you are walking down the street, I want you to hold your head high and look at every fucking person you see out there and say to yourself, 'I ain't like the rest of you motherfuckers.' Exactly like that. 'Motherfucker, I'm different!' You saved American POWs. You ain't like everybody else."

"What, I'm supposed to change the way I view myself, just like that?"

"Yes, Elliot, just like that. Not a week from now, not in a month, not in a year, right fucking now!"

"Just like that?"

"Just . . . like . . . that! Change the way you think, today. Buddy, you saved American POWs. Are you kidding me? That's unreal. Today, start being proud that you're different."

You know what he did? He showed up to Unbreakable the very next day, a totally different man. He made the decision to change the way he viewed himself and to give himself permission to love himself up, which most of us suck at. Obviously, he still had pain. He still had work to do to come back from the physical and psychological trauma of what he'd been through in war and in homecoming. But like I've said, and I'll say again, there's no more powerful weapon on the planet than what's between our ears. By changing his perspective about himself—and his service, his injury, his scars—he fucking changed EVERYTHING. Oh, and by the way, now Elliot greets everyone who walks into Unbreakable with the biggest smile in the room. He has become a leader inside MVP and someone we all rely upon seven days a week. Elliot kicks ass now in the workplace. He's a dad. He's simply an amazing man. He's serving others just as much now, or perhaps even more, after his uniform came off. He has helped so many of our vets, has saved countless lives. Elliot has a knack for knowing when a member of MVP is down and calling them to give them emotional support and lift them out of the dark shadow Elliott used to live in.

Oh, and by the way, Elliot and his unit didn't save just any American POWs. The POW the bad guys were trying to get back that day was Shoshana Johnson, the first ever female African American POW in the history of our country! I had the privilege of meeting her on an MVP session, where she was re-united with Elliot and the other Marines who'd rescued her, for the very first time since that event. They never got to meet, be-cause she had been medevacked out, and they went back to fight. And then, all of them went about their lives after the military. She actually got to thank them, face to face, for the first time ever . . . all because Elliot changed the way he viewed himself. He became active in MVP, and in turn helped to build MVP, and it was through MVP that the reunion happened. When ninety-seven of us at MVP watched that reunion go down, there wasn't a dry eye in sight. Holy shit were we all crying our eyes out. Shoshana, if you are reading this, you are absolutely amazing in every way.

In June of 2021, Elliot actually drove to El Paso to meet Shoshana in person. After that meeting, he came to MVP and declared: "We forget too often that we are heroes to a lot of people. We really do need to be proud of the things we do a lot more. I would never have seen how special I really am without this team. Everyone on our team needs to start realizing, right now, how special we really are."

Just as I explained the concept of loyalty in Chapter 2, so too are teams a give-give relationship. Teams must be built on us giving and giving, not always taking and taking. For exam-ple, my fight teams beat the hell out of me. I beat the hell out of them. Yet, we give-give in ways most people probably can't comprehend. I've been on numerous fight teams over the years, and in between punches and kicks, I've been able to open up to my teammates in a way I might not have been able to do over a beer. Being made to feel raw and hurt in the cage was actually cathartic and allowed me to be raw and talk about how I was hurting too.

The day I found out I was getting divorced, I was at Arizona Combat Sports, training with my friend and teammate Jesse Forbes, who at the time was competing in the UFC. I walked in, pale and out of it, and he asked if maybe we wanted to hold off on training.

"Fuckkkkk no, I want to go!"

Training was the most therapeutic thing for me. And as tired as we both may have been, he knew I needed this, in the same way I needed him and his full-throttle support.

Another time, one of my teammates was training to fight for the lightweight championship of the world. I tore my calf and was supposed to be out for eight weeks. But I was back in eight days, so I could give him a look from a shorter southpaw, because that's what he needed to prepare for his fight. I couldn't fight much because my calf was torn, but I was able to give him some help in fight prep. The point is this: go above and beyond for your teammates. Unrelenting support—regardless of your mood—should be one of the tentpole ideals of your team. Showing up to support your teammates, even when you're hurting, gives a team more value. Do it for your teammates, and they'll do it for you, and you'll both benefit, in the receiving, and in the giving, and especially in the knowledge that you have people you can rely on in your life.

My son, Sammy, is one of the absolute core members of my team. I wanted to give him roots, a foundation, and love. One thing that makes our team even more special is: we chose each other! I didn't know you could love another human this much until I met him. But the fact that we chose each other makes our team even more special. We are devoted to being on each other's team! I tell my son I love him a million times a day. He will never grow up saying he was never told that. That was my job as a dad and a team member. His job as my son was to just . . . be my son. We need to be more openminded/flexible in how we define and build our families and our teams. When we feel that special connection, we should follow our hearts, no matter the obstacles or the fact that it doesn't necessarily make sense to everyone else.

Sammy has had a funny life, growing up around our other family: Strahan, Bradshaw, Howie, Jimmy, and Curt. By the way, we are totally not cool in his eyes. Oh, it's deflating. They are all just his "uncool" uncles in his mind. But they are all my family, my team, and one I can rely on greatly. You all see us out there on TV, laughing and hooting and having fun, but what you don't know is how much I lean on that team for my mental health. Every single February, when the NFL season ends, I go through a rough patch between my ears because I'm not around them anymore. Howie Long makes it a point to check up on me since I've told him how hard it gets for me without that team.

It's not just my FOX crew, but the entire NFL that makes up my team. Four years ago, I was on my annual forty-day NFL Training Camp Tour when Dan Quinn, then the head coach of the Atlanta Falcons, asked me why I'm still traveling around, from team to team, like I did when I started those tours in 1999. Now, as I did then, I go to each team for about thirty-six to forty-eight hours, then pop over to the next one. Oh, and I do it with nothing but carry-on bags (it's not like I need to check bags for my haircare products).

"Man, don't you get tired of living out of a suitcase for forty straight days, and haven't you kind of gone up and beyond all this at this point?" he asked. He thought that with *Ballers* taking off the way it had, and my role with FOX becoming even more personality driven, and all of the endorsements I was getting, I didn't need to do this same grind I'd done when I started covering the NFL on TV in 1999.

"Noooooo!" I exclaimed. "There's no moving up and beyond from all of you! You guys have been my social structure for all these years, my therapists, some of you feel like family. There's no moving 'up and on' from that, and from all of you. I need that bond, man, for my own mental health."

Later that night, at dinner, I revealed to him how much I struggle, how much the whole league means to me and explained how this premise of my needing a team was the basis for MVP. I didn't hold back.

It resonated with him so much that you know what he did that night? He donated $100,000 and opened up the Atlanta chapter of MVP on the spot! There's so much good in that sentence! Quinn has attended the Atlanta chapter, in person, and the LA sessions, regularly via Zoom. When he got fired as head coach of the Falcons, he went into a dark hole and leaned on MVP, and it was there for him.

"This is the first time I've been in transition in my life," Quinn, now the defensive coordinator of the Dallas Cowboys, told the seventy veterans and players on one of the MVP calls, about three weeks after his firing. "I never knew how hard it actually would be, and thank God, I had this crew to help me through those dark patches. You've needed me, and now I need you. I am really proud to be part of this team. You all can't imagine how much you've lifted me up at times when I didn't know how down I was."

Now THAT is what I'm talking about, teammate. THAT is why we build our teams. You never know when we are going to need that lift. You invite other people to join your team, simply by being honest about how much you need that team for your own mental health, and by sharing that you know, from your own experience, how many other people in their orbit are relying on their team too. This vulnerability gives others a chance to help you, and to acknowledge when they need help too. Then, you can lift them up, and you all save each other—not only supporting each other, but literally saving lives—one big happy mafia.

Teams don't only have to come in the form of people. I adopted a rescue pit bull, Alma. She was horrifically abused before being rescued, then she lived in a shelter for three and a half years. Nobody wanted to adopt her because of all her scars. However, it was her scars that I felt made her so beautiful. She has become my emotional support dog, and I'm her emotional support human. Win-win, we love each other up, along with all our scars.

You know who else is on my team? God. Yup, that one, up there.

As you can tell, I talk a lot, and a lot of that has been to constantly distract myself from the lack of love and worth I had in myself. Being left by myself was never pretty, always painful. At an early age, during one of my nightly crying spells in bed (they happened every single night), I just started talking to God. Nobody taught it to me, I just felt it. And talk and talk and talk I did. I still am. I guess you can call it praying, but in my prayers, I'm not only telling God what's happening in my life. I am asking how God is doing as well. I pray that God feels the love many of us give, that God is having a great day, or that God is enjoying life. Even this is a give-give relationship. I find myself talking to God all the time. The ADD probably helps with that, but it's also my way of attacking the feelings of loneliness that the gray can produce. So, when I am all alone, I talk or pray or meditate, or whatever you want to call it. I look up or sometimes shut my eyes and just talk to God.

By the way, I view God as, of course, God, but also as serving the role of my parent and best friend. And just like my parents and friends want the best for me, I believe God does as well. Even though I feel as if God is always there for me, I also feel I control a lot of my destiny. I have to help myself, not just rely on God, or any other teammate, to make it all happen for me. That's the whole "God helps those who help themselves" deal.

Oh, and there's one more big thing I believe. I don't view God as this punishing, judge-y figure. I know many of us have been taught that if we don't follow certain religious rules, we'll be punished. I simply don't believe God sits there and waits for us to mess up. I think God has compassion and empathy and, just as a parent would, hopes we can right our wrongs and become better versions of ourselves. I have had a best friend–type parent with me for every up and down, high and low. All because I CHOOSE to believe that someone up there loves me. I wake up each morning, saying "I love you" back. That is way better than me just waking up and seeing how shitty the gray is.

I don't need to see an actual tangible physical thing in front of my face to believe it's there. I am still single, but I have faith that I will find love, and love will find me. This decision to have faith has already helped lead me to many dreams coming true, especially in my career. It allowed me to rise above the fear of failure and the equally gripping fear of the unknown. So, as a result, I've never felt 100 percent completely alone, even when I was rejected and dejected. This helped me continue to rise up, to be relentless in climbing the ladder of sports, broadcasting, business, and life.

The praying led me to read a lot of prayer books, and I would take what I could and apply it to my life. God has laid out some pretty cool things for us . . . if we want to see them. For example, this is a lesson I've used as much as any in my life. It's right there in the Ten Commandments (by the way, there's only ten of them, so before we all bitch and moan about how shitty the world is, I wonder how shitty it would be if we all followed these ten SIMPLE rules. Simple. Don't murder anyone, don't freakin' steal, don't bang your neighbor's spouse . . . they shouldn't be THAT hard).

The Fourth Commandment, most of us don't follow, maybe you can't even remember which one that is. I, however, have followed it to the core. You know which one I'm talking about? God is commanding us to take a day off, have a Sabbath, refresh our bodies and our souls, and spend time with loved ones. Imagine that novel idea. God is saying to us, "Dude, chillllllllll." Not commanding us to give away our money, or not enjoy ourselves or sacrifice anything. Oh, and by the way, part of the commandment is to take the day off and drink some wine. Well, gee, God, don't threaten me with a good time. I took that day off, or Sabbath, to heart.

Take, for example, those ten years of me being broke as fuck, trying to get a full-time job, and facing daily butt-whippings, and rejections, and disappointments. Friday night would come and . . . I'd . . . relaxxxxxxx. Breathe in. . . . exhaleeee. No matter what had happened that week, it was over, done, kaput. I could wipe away the week behind me, relax for a day, and then start up my fight again with a whole new clean slate.

"God, I'm not asking you to make sure I get a job or get

some windfall of money. I'm not even asking you to make sure I don't get knocked down. All I'm asking is that when I do get knocked down, help me pick myself up, help me brush myself off, and let's continue to walk this walk together!"

The week that was? It's over. Everything that happened, it's done. I got a clean slate. You know what, thank you, my best friend, God, for giving me the understanding and insight to give my soul a break.

I started doing this in 1989, and I didn't get a full-time, paying job that didn't go Chapter 11 until 1999. That is a full decade of rejection and heartbreak. A DECADE! But I didn't view it as ten years of being told I wasn't good enough or being told I wasn't getting hired. I viewed it as a series of one-week periods of rejection that happened to go on for a decade. If I didn't have faith in the first place I never would have read those passages. Had I not read those passages I likely would have given up well before the ten-year mark.

Look at this, I've found teams with God, the NFL, *Fox NFL Sunday*, pop stars, fight teams, my son, my dog, veterans, and more. I know I'm writing all this to help guide and coach you, teammate. But I also stated from the first pages of this book, I needed you to walk this walk by my side, for me, as much as for you. Wow, reading these words . . . I'm trying to be very real and raw here . . . it's long been hard for me to see all this love, but right here, on this paper, yeah, my teams . . . I am surrounded by love. When you're in the gray that's hard to see. Right now, I see it clearer than I ever have.

That's why, these teams, they are one of the central pillars of how to take the gray and tap it out, or at least win some rounds on the scorecards. When you combine the mantra "Have a Team" with my other two pillars, "Be of Service" and "Use

Laughter to Fight the Gray," suddenly we get to see a whole lot more streaks of blue. The gray looks at all of that and starts to ask itself, "What happened to the sad, depressed person I could control? Where did he go?"

That's how we fight back. That's how we live in the blue. We all DESERVE to live in the blue.

Let's circle back to the first team I wrote about in this chapter. Unbreakable. Not only is Unbreakable an actual physical place, but there is a mindset to being Unbreakable. It's a mindset I've used to not only get through the gray, but I've also used it to push athletes, performers, all kinds of people to greatness. I'm going to show you how in the next two chapters, all as a way to unleash your own Unbreakable power.

Just as I did when I pulled back the curtain and showed you what it's like inside MVP, over these next two chapters I will pull back another curtain and show you what makes up the Unbreakable Mindset. You're on our team now, you're coming with us.

TEAMMATE, LET ME ASK YOU:

Beyond me, and the pages of this book, do you have a team? If so, are you doing right by those on your team? Are you checking in on your teammates? Are you showing up by being authentic and vulnerable about your own shit? Having a team is a gift. Use it! If you don't have a team, my friend, you need one—probably more than one—ASAP, if you're going to be Unbreakable. I challenge you to not just reach for the easiest team either (though I want you to reach for them as well). A team of your colleagues, your neighbors, people at your places of worship, that's great too! I have those kinds of teams. But dare to build a team that's like what Unbreakable and MVP are for me. Not a place filled with celebrities. That's not what I'm talking about, and I know that's certainly not the norm. But rather places where you can be your most real and fucked up and broken, and you can be of service to the people who need it the most. BECAUSE THE TEAM THAT CHALLENGES YOU IS THE ONE THAT GROWS YOU.

9

THE UNBREAKABLE MINDSET, PART ONE

Unbreakable is a mindset. It's an attitude. It's a code I teach and a creed I coach and live my life by . . . both inside the cage *and* outside it. I use it in business dealings, at my NFL Insider job, in my charity. It's this attitude that allows me to be relentless in pursuit of my goals, step out of the ordinary, and reach for my dreams. Make those dreams come true, and experience "how the fuck did I get here?" moments that go way beyond what I could have dreamed.

I first got involved in combat sports training in 1982 as a twelve-year-old wrestler on my grade-school team. Then, as a teenager in the late '80s, I began boxing and studied many forms of martial arts. In 2000, mixed martial arts got its hooks into me. I had two professional fights in 2003, back when they used to pit different styles of martial arts against each other, to see which was the superior style. My first day at 21st Century FOX Studios, after signing a lucrative deal with FOX Sports, I came limping in, peppered with bruises, after winning three matches in ninety minutes at a massive submission fighting tournament a day earlier. The FOX executives took one look at me, found out about the competition, and immediately told me, "You will never ever, ever, fucking do that again!"

"By never . . . do you mean . . . ?"

"Fucking NEVER!" barked a FOX executive.

But I won! Talk about zero fanfare.

Still, I couldn't stop. Fighting was more useful for my mental health than the countless antidepressant pills that doctors had prescribed for me over the years. So, I figured out how to use the Fox brass's declaration to my advantage. They told me I couldn't fight, but they never said I couldn't train or coach others. There is *never* an end of the road, gang. *Never*. But you have to decide that and follow through with conviction.

So, in 2006, I started the first mixed martial arts cross-training program for professional athletes. I have trained more than a thousand pro athletes in MMA over a fifteen-year span. I started with Chiefs and Vikings All-Pro Jared Allen and have gone on to train stars like Patrick Willis, Clay Matthews, Bobby Wagner, Andrew Whitworth, Odell Beckham Jr. I've even trained full teams, like the Saints, for six weeks; the Falcons, twice; the Rams; the Browns—the list goes on and on. I have since coached this method to countless athletes, business leaders, pop stars, and actors and actresses at Unbreakable and throughout the world.

And now, I have the honor of teaching this same mindset to you, teammate, using the five pillars of the Unbreakable Mindset.

This is not just another take on the same old tips about how to be a better athlete, or a more focused person. These are the insider techniques I've used to take all levels of people and push them to life-changing greatness. This is how we create warriors. You all have it in you!

I. Find out who the best is . . . and do more than them.

II. Be relentless.

III. Push your breaking point, push your breaking point, push your breaking point.

IV. Neutral face: don't ever show you're hurt or tired.

V. It's your honor to fight hurt.

PILLAR I: FIND OUT WHO THE BEST IS . . . AND DO MORE THAN THEM.

It's literally that simple, teammate. Find out where you want to be in life and do more than everyone else to get there. Outwork the world. That's the big magic bullet for success. Seriously. It's right there in front of your face.

Don't just believe me. Go look into the lives of the Tom Bradys, Peyton Mannings, Jerry Rices, Derek Jeters, Michael Jordans, Tiger Woodses, Lindsey Vonns of the sports world. Or people like Jeff Bezos, Dr. Dre, Steve Jobs, Mark Cuban, Oprah, The Rock, Guy Fieri (people from all walks of life who have built business empires). Many of them were rejected multiple times, and for many years, on their way to greatness. But their work ethic didn't allow them to lie down because of the rejection.

I have been blessed to be around greatness, in the form of Bradshaw, Long, Stallone, Dwayne, Guy Fieri, and so many others. I've learned by observing them closely and asking them how they did it. And it's pretty damn cool that I get to pass their lessons on to you. Again, just because you don't have any

A-listers on your team doesn't mean that you don't have people in your life who could be mentors. Or pick someone you admire in any field, and research what makes them the best. With the internet and social media, we've got greater access to the legends of our day than ever before. I'm not just teaching you lessons that have worked for me. I'm showing you how to look out for wisdom in your own life. We can all learn from each other.

Let's take the success route of one of my closest friends, Hall of Fame tight end Tony Gonzalez. Hey, I don't just use him as the butt of my jokes, I learn from him as well. In seventeen years in the NFL, he was considered the greatest tight end in the history of pro football. The greatest means Number 1! How amazing must that feel? To be the Number 1 who has ever done it, in the history of all time?

What you may not remember, even if you're a die-hard NFL fan, is that Tony was benched his rookie year. Sent to go sit down with the backups, he led the league in dropped passes, couldn't stay on the field. By his own admission, he was terrible his first two years and certainly wasn't reliable. Two seasons he wished he could forget. He was so depressed, he started isolating himself in his home, drinking way too much booze, and thinking like a loser, as opposed to a winner.

He had a decision to make. Life is about our decisions. We can keep doing the same thing over and over and "hope it changes," which would have likely led to Tony being a colossal bust. Or we can make a change.

The change Tony made? He found out who was the best, and he decided to outwork them, not by a little, but by a huge margin. He did *exactly* what I am trying to teach you here. He focused on learning as much as he could by reading, watching videos, whatever information he could glean on diet, sleep, training, studying. His work ethic was unparalleled.

Tony went from catching about ten or fifteen balls every practice, like everyone else in his position, to catching, get this, as he told me: "Between seventy-five and a hundred before practice, one hundred fifty during practice when the defense was going, and fifty to seventy-five after. All of this with my chinstrap buckled, mouthpiece in, eyes wide open like I would in a game. I tucked the ball as quickly as possible after the catch too. Put your mind in the same place it will be during a game."

Every . . . single . . . day! He made the Pro Bowl that year, in his third season, as well as thirteen of the next fourteen Pro Bowls. He went on to catch more passes, for more yards and more touchdowns, than any other player at his position in the history of the National Football League. In 2019 he was inducted into the Pro Football Hall of Fame, where he talked about what a colossal failure he was when he first came into the league. But he had the desire to change, and outworking the world was his recipe for doing so.

In fact, in his eleventh NFL training camp I got his head coach to give him a pass on curfew, so he could actually go out on the town with me. It was training camp and his Chiefs were getting ready for a preseason game that Tony wasn't going to play in (many teams rest their best players in the preseason). So, on my one night in River Falls, Wisconsin—the longtime home of the Chiefs' training camp—the team's coach was giving Tony a pass, as a favor to me, so I wouldn't have to rush dinner. Yet Gonzalez refused, because despite him not playing in that next day's game, he wanted to wake up at six a.m. to train and catch balls.

If you want greatness in any area or field, this pillar represents the straightest path to getting there and living your dream.

Let me jump to another field. Wiz Khalifa, a member of Unbreakable since 2016, is a rapper, songwriter, and pop star. His song "Black and Yellow" hit No. 1 on the US Billboard Hot 100, and his song with Charlie Puth, "See You Again," was the most streamed track, in one week, in the history of Spotify, and the most downloaded song of 2015. What you don't know is, to get here, Wiz went the same route as Gonzalez. You see the fame now, but what you haven't seen are the countless shows he put on in front of zero guests. That's not a typo. ZERO. Countless shows, with three people watching, five people watching, and, yeah, there was a gig at a swim club with an audience of zero. How many of you are willing to stand in front of zero people and perform? How many of you would be so discouraged, you wouldn't ever put on another show? Or would just complain that nobody showed up? Instead, Wiz kept at it, booking as many of those gigs as he could, working at his craft, more than everybody else. Think about that, performing at swim clubs . . . where nobody came to watch . . . but staying the course, month after month, year after year, to reach his dreams.

The true sign of greatness is the work you put in when nobody is watching. When nobody is pushing or demanding that you finish a set or workout. It's the hours you spend, by yourself, training, studying, watching film, practicing, working on your craft.

One of the best lines I ever heard came from quarterback Drew Brees on a night when I crashed his solitude. (Yeah, I have no boundaries.)

His coach, Sean Payton, and I were in downtown New Orleans on a Thursday night around ten p.m. I was about eight cocktails in when suddenly Sean rained on my parade. He'd forgotten something in his office and made my ass ride with him *all* the way back out to the Saints' facility to grab whatever it was.

When we walked inside, every single light was off . . . except one. Sitting alone, in a meeting room, with film on and notes in front of him was Brees.

Ten forty-five at night. All alone.

"Dude, what the fuck ya doing?" I asked, shocked at what I'd stumbled upon.

Brees shrugged and delivered the greatest, unintentional motivational line I've ever heard in my life: "Sometimes trying to be great is lonely."

How cool is THAT? Sometimes trying to be great is lonely.

What a line . . . To which I somewhat jokingly responded, "Holy shit, I am so stealing that from you."

Every other player had fled the Saints facility by about four p.m. that day . . . or nearly *seven hours* earlier. But there was Brees, by himself in a pitch-black building, trying to outwork the world with nobody watching. Just like he did most days. How'd that consistent level of commitment turn out for him? Welp, all he's done since is . . . go on to throw more touchdowns than any other player in the history of the NFL, not to mention holding the records for career pass completions, career completion percentage, and career passing yards; all this, despite being shorter than the vast majority of his counterparts in modern football history. It's not as if Brees is bigger, more gifted, more athletic. He's not. Not by a mile. He just OUT-WORKS them ALL.

It has to be your decision to want to put this kind of work in because work means sacrifice. I was once having a conversation with an NFL defensive end about the incredible success of star perennial Pro Bowler J. J. Watt. I will leave the player's name out of this, but I still remember the conversation vividly.

"Man, look at what J.J. has done, man," he said. "We came out in the same draft around the same grade, but he's just blown past me. I don't understand it."

"Well, look at his work ethic," I replied. "Look at how hard that fucker works. If you want to be great find out what he does for his workout and preparation routine and do more than him."

Oh, you'll love his response.

"More than him? Are you crazy? Do you see how much that guy does? I can't do more than him."

Ummm, huh?

"Well dude, you just answered your own question about why he's been able to thrive and why you haven't matched him."

"Oh, yeah, what he does is crazy. I can't do that."

Hey, I tried. He had a chance at greatness. These guys we train, all of them, they have a chance at greatness. We all do. I never thought I'd have the ability, or the platform, or anything close to what they've accomplished as athletes. I had to fucking fight, long and hard, to get here. No matter what you're doing . . . live it, breathe it, go above and beyond.

Whenever I sit with a new player who comes to me to train, during that very first meeting, I always interject this: "When you're done playing, and your career is over, and that glass closes on your team photo for the rest of your life, who the fuck do you want people to see? Do you want them to see a guy who played in the NFL? Or do you want them to see greatness? Much of it is up to you."

Outwork the world, it's worth it.

PILLAR II: BE RELENTLESS.

Now that we've armed you with an understanding of a better workload, let's add to your arsenal: the art of a relentless pace. It's the most effective offensive weapon you can have in your toolkit.

Pace is everything. I try to teach my fighters and players, "Be a torrential downpour of aggression." Bring the heat so it just . . . doesn't . . . stop! And it never slows.

Relentless, relentless, relentless. Whether we are talking about being in the ring or building a business, constantly apply pressure, move forward, apply more pressure, move forward . . . then ramp the pace up even more relentlessly, until our opponent says, "HOLY FUCK . . . GET THIS MOTHERFUCKER OFF ME! I'M DONE!" You always want to set the pace—make the other person keep up with you—instead of reacting to them. By doing so, you're automatically in charge—of the play, of the negotiation, of the conversation.

Whenever I preach the gospel of the Unbreakable Mindset to NFL teams, I start them all off the same: "When that game starts . . . view it like that cage door slamming shut, and you better make those men across from you BEG to get out of the cage with you! Make it a horrible afternoon for your opponents. Win or lose, your goal is to make them admit that day absolutely sucked for them. Lock that cage door behind them!"

So, how do you make them beg to get out of that cage or off that field? Ramp that relentless pace up on them, so much that they aren't willing to match it . . . and then sprinkle in some, oh, I don't know, how about . . . ummmm . . . even more relentlessness.

"Make everything hurt on the man across from you," I tell

our athletes. "Every time you put your hands on them make it hurt. Every time they put their hands on you? Make that hurt them too! Then ramp that pace up on them yet again."

A beautiful cycle is created. Your opponent gets tired, you ramp up the pace, while at the same time, you don't show your own level of fatigue. They get more exhausted, and when you realize it, you ramp up even more, and you forget your own pain. Then when the time is right, you start throwing bombs. Don't try to squeak out a decision. Go for the knockout. Go for the finish. I know I'm sounding a little Cobra Kai–ish here, but the lessons herein are meant for *victory* in sport, life, and business.

Yes, business. Using this principle is how I became an NFL Insider, grinding relentlessly for a decade of penniless years, until I finally got my first full-time gig for CBS Sports' *The NFL Today*. I didn't stop there. I have been absolutely relentless in my pursuit to build Unbreakable into a multimillion-dollar brand with reach far beyond our physical gym. I used this same relentlessness to build MVP to become a multicity, nationwide, nonprofit charity. And I am relentless in convincing others why they should believe and jump aboard our bandwagon.

In January of 2020, I signed on to become the new spokesman for GNC. With that role GNC also gave me my own Unbreakable line of protein powders and shakes, amino acids, preworkout powders and more. In my very first dinner meeting, with Josh Burris, the man who would soon become their CEO, they told me their plans to start with vanilla and chocolate flavors.

"Vanilla? I've never done anything vanilla in my life," I said.

That statement sold Josh on the fact that I was going to push harder and be a more relentless partner than they'd probably expected. I didn't stop there. The very next day, in their board room, as they started giving me flavors, I actually pushed back.

"Nope, there's nothing different about it. I need this to be different."

The nerve, right? Everyone in the room sat in stunned disbelief. Until, finally, someone said, "I'm glad he's pushing the group. Yes, it's time to be different."

Over the course of the next few months, I asked them to send me sample after sample after sample. I was relentless in our pursuit of being special, until . . . *BAM* . . . I found the versions of those flavors that I absolutely loved. I am so incredibly proud of this line and our potential for future growth. Oh, and by the way, that attitude got Burris and GNC to jump aboard the MVP bandwagon and pledge a whopping $1 million in our first year of partnership. Had I just sat there and not interjected what I really thought, I don't believe any of that would have happened. Yes, this was that relentless attitude at work.

Relentless, relentless, relentless. Pace, pace, pace. If this sounds exhausting as you're reading it . . . good! Point proven. That's what's going to earn you one of the spots at the top of whatever you're trying to do, teammate. But I can't just *tell* you or anyone else to simply be relentless. It must be learned and practiced, which you can do only by building on the next three lessons of the Unbreakable Mindset.

PILLAR III: PUSH YOUR BREAKING POINT.

A lot of people don't realize what they're capable of . . . not even close . . . even fucking champions. I'm in the business of taking people beyond where they ever thought they could go.

I say, "Push your breaking point to build new foundations and reach new heights." Having upped my breaking point at the gym, I've shown myself that I'm capable of much more. Knowing I have greater depths of physical and mental perseverance pushes my ceiling of what I can accomplish in business . . . and every other area of life as well.

When I opened Unbreakable, I was using totally different muscles than I had as a sports reporter and NFL Insider. Suddenly, I had to hire people, manage people, discipline people, fire people. The buck stopped with me. There were plenty of times I was outside my comfort zone. This is the chaos I live in, trying to juggle all the moving business parts of my life: in one day, I had to set up separate training for Demi Lovato, Joe Jonas, and Nick Jonas, all of whom were touring, while I was at NFL training camp practice with the 49ers.

Picture this: I am watching practice and making calls in between plays to make sure everyone we sent on the road was following our protocol and also respecting the privacy of those stars. Those texts were going out around other texts to our Unbreakable GM, to make sure I properly handled issues that had arisen in the gym that morning . . . and were also done while I was trying to meet with the 49ers executives to pump up MVP to them as potential donors. So yes, I had to train myself to be good in chaos in the gym first, because for me that allows me to be good in chaos while handling business—and everything else.

There's a particular drill I use in my gym that epitomizes this strategy.

I call it the 30, 30, 30 Drill. There's anywhere from three to twelve minutes of work, but every thirty seconds I'll have you change up what you are doing. For example, I may have you hitting the heavy bag for thirty seconds, then sprinting on the bag for thirty, then kicking for thirty, then sprawls, then knees, and so forth.

In a game everything changes up, every ten seconds, or every thirty seconds. In fights things change every five seconds or so. In pretty much anything, shit changes quickly. It's the same in all areas of life, especially with how much gets thrown at us these days on our phones. You gotta have flexibility, quick reflexes, and be extremely willing to adjust.

Back to that drill, I usually start them with one three-minute round, their first time in. That's to establish their initial baseline. I do three exercises, thirty seconds each, then go back through them again. That's a hundred eighty seconds, or three minutes. The next week, I will add in one additional movement or drill (four different drills, thirty seconds each). I have them complete that twice, without stopping, so the round goes to four minutes. As the weeks go by, I go to a five-minute round, then two four-minute rounds, then a seven-minute round, and up and up it goes. Every time we increase the workload, I make sure I not only point out how a single three-minute round was incredibly difficult for them when we originally started our training. I also make sure they are proud of how much their breaking point has moved.

Always reward and celebrate growth, teammate . . . always.

By the time I send my NFL players back to training camp, they're doing a ten- or twelve-minute round. But what's even more important is not their improved cardiovascular health, although that's fucking badass. It's their new Unbreakable Mindset. I'll say to them, "Remember, guys, two months ago, you came in here, you had a hard time getting through three minutes? Now, you're used to twelve freaking minutes of this, and you crushed it. Anytime you think you're tired on the football field, I want you to think back and go, 'I'm not fucking tired. This is nothing. That twelve-minute 30, 30, 30, now that was exhausting. I'm good to go.'"

Let me throw one more drill at you before we move on. I named this drill Finish the Fight. I came up with this drill after I saw two friends of mine fight for world titles, hurt their opponents, and unload their whole gas tank to go for that win. In both cases, their opponents survived that onslaught and fought to come back. Problem is, my two friends had already punched themselves out. They left it all in that round and were unable to mount much of an offense the rest of the fight, and both would go on to lose.

As a result, I came up with a drill to prepare for this, to push their breaking points to where they can completely unload their arsenal—yet recover if needed. So, for the drill, I have our fighters work the heavy bag for five-minute rounds. About ten times in those five minutes I will yell out, "You hurt him! You hurt him! Finish the fight!" I'll have them absolutely unload for about eight to ten seconds, then, step, sprawl, and jump back up, as if the round is continuing. The sprawl was inserted because, in many cases, when an MMA fighter is hurt, their default is to try to shoot a takedown. A sprawl defends against this. You see what I'm doing here? I am training them to push their breaking point several times, per round, while conditioning their bodies to recover in order to keep the pressure ramped up.

By changing their reality with both of these drills, I can also change their perceptions of what was hard, which, in turn, changes their mindset about how far they can go.

Think about how valuable this lesson is. Think of the inner currency this builds up in your soul. Confidence that your breaking point is further than those around you, or those you are competing against, is the magic bullet that can overcome doubt, take greatness to the next level, and make you Unbreakable, for keeps.

This all leads to the final two pillars of the Unbreakable Mindset.

TEAMMATE LET ME ASK YOU:

Are you as great as you could be? Welp, I can answer that. Unless you're one of the six examples I gave in this chapter of people who are literally doing EVERYTHING they can in their pursuit of greatness, you're probably not. Most of us aren't. But here's the thing. You have the chance to be Unbreakable. Today. What's the area you care about the most? Your health? Your career? Your family? Start with one. Who is the best person you know, or you've read about, in this area? What do they do to be great? Now, do that, plus one! And then, do it again tomorrow. And as soon as you see any improvement, love yourself up for it, and then, work even fucking harder. BECAUSE I CAN SEE: YOU ARE UNBREAKABLE.

THE UNBREAKABLE MINDSET, PART TWO

The Unbreakable Mindset isn't just about how you beat your opponent down on the field, in a business meeting, or wherever you need to triumph. It's also about all the skills you sharpen to prepare for the game, and especially the ways you talk to yourself in your head. That's what Part Two of the Unbreakable Mindset is all about: the long game, and how to *keep* yourself in a position to play, and to win, no matter the obstacles.

PILLAR IV: NEUTRAL FACE: DON'T EVER SHOW YOU'RE HURT OR TIRED.

Let's begin with a story:

Randy Couture could barely lift his hands. In case you've never heard of him, he's the UFC Hall of Famer and former light heavyweight and heavyweight champion of the world. The guy with the crazy cauliflower ears, who starred as one of *The Expendables* in the Sly Stallone franchise. *That* Randy Couture.

He was staggering around the cage, the entire arena warped in a dizzying spiral . . . from his depth perception severely shutting down. He was on the edge of losing consciousness. He was so tired that his brain was telling him to move forward, but his body was telling him to fuck off; he wasn't sure which to listen to.

What his opponent, Mike VanArsdale, didn't know was, going into their fight, Randy was battling a brutal, dangerous staph infection that prevented him from training properly for six weeks. But this was back in the days when MMA was still battling for its spot in mainstream sports, and fighters had very little financial security. If you didn't fight, you didn't get paid. Randy needed to fight, to get his yearly average salary (which wasn't much).

He was so sick that he had a PICC line pumping antibiotics into his vein. But he wasn't about to let his opponent know any of this. So, right before the fight—and remember, this man had not trained *right* for six weeks—he pulled the PICC out and then went to go fight.

Over the years, I have had Randy repeat this story to nearly all of the more than one thousand pro athletes we have trained together. He always delivers the punch line, just like this: "That was the most exhausted I've ever been in *my entire life*. Just, holy shit, was I exhausted! I walked over to my stool, and I felt like I was going to pass out. But I turned around and saw Mike plop down, exhausted, on his stool. So, I made myself wink and smile at him, to get him to think I had a ton more in the tank, and that we were just getting started."

That's right. Even though Randy had every reason to go sit down and rest after the round, he refused to take a stool for the full one-minute break leading up to round three. Instead, he watched VanArsdale breathing heavily, gasping for air, revealing his complete and utter exhaustion. Clocking all this, Randy bounced up and down, and sent that smile and wink his way.

In reality, as soon as Randy had done that, the fight was over. When the next round started, even though VanArsdale was standing across from Randy in that cage, he wasn't really there. Nope. He'd checked out on that stool. All because of a smile and a wink.

Fifty-one seconds later, Randy choked VanArsdale out. Three quick taps of the hand by VanArsdale, signaling he'd had enough. The fight was over and now Randy's hand was raised . . . the hand of the very same arm in which he had had the IV PICC line just before.

Imagine how ridiculous this is—that a fighter who had had a staph infection and couldn't train for weeks was still able to find something different between his ears and behind his rib cage to win the spot of Number 1 contender in the light heavyweight division. Randy's body language hurt VanArsdale, exponentially more than his punches, kicks, and slams did.

This epitomizes the Unbreakable Mindset. But before you say, "Wait I'm not built like Randy Couture, I couldn't possibly do that," remember that Randy didn't use physical strength to win that fight. In fact, he was incredibly weak during the eleven minutes it took for him to end it. The most tired he'd ever felt during competition, as he recalled. While VanArsdale was physically training, Randy was preparing his heart and mind, and those, if trained right, will always be stronger than muscles.

A couple of years ago (around a decade after that fight and years after Randy and I had started our MMA training program for pro athletes striving to become Unbreakable), *Sports*

Illustrated featured us in an article about our program. I told the story of Randy's fight with VanArsdale, as the epitome of the Unbreakable Mindset.

Not long after the piece ran, I got a call from Rashad Evans, the former UFC Light Heavyweight Champion of the World, who was training with VanArsdale at the time.

"Dude, you don't know what you did," he said.

"What? What did I do?" I asked, really thinking to myself, *Uh, oh, what the fuck did I do this time?!?*

"You broke Mike's heart. For all these years, he never knew that Randy had a staph infection. He thought the other way around. Randy was so strong, Mike thought he was actually juicing. Yeah, you just broke his heart."

Well, I had to go ahead and break it . . . just a little bit more. "All that dude had to do was come running off his stool and throw bombs, and Randy would've been done, and Mike would have gotten a title shot," I told Rashad.

In the end, it wasn't punches, or double-leg takedowns, or Randy's notorious ground-and-pound technique that won that fight. Randy broke VanArsdale with a wink, a smile, and a face that showed zero fatigue or pain, despite the fact he was about to pass out. That was all it took for VanArsdale to become convinced, *Fuck this. There's no way I can beat that guy.*

During his UFC career, Randy won at least three fights using this same method, including one against the equally legendary Chuck Liddell, a hall of fame world champion with the most knockouts in UFC history in the light heavyweight division. Randy did it to Chuck, oh by the way, while hiding the fact that he was fighting with an injured leg. Chuck had zero idea Randy wasn't at full strength. Zero clue. Randy never showed it, even though he was in a world of pain. Then his pain became glory when he was crowned UFC Light Heavyweight Champion of the World. We're talking about Chuck Fucking Liddell, one of the most legendary champions of all times. Chuck is so scary, he won a fight in a ring staged in the middle of the jungle in Brazil . . . one twenty-five-minute round, bareknuckle, no holds barred, no rules, $3,500, winner take all. Yeah, my friends are . . . ummmm . . . different.

Just as Randy did to VanArsdale, he wore Chuck out, and in between rounds, kept looking at him. He smiled, winked, seemingly getting stronger, and never let Chuck know that he was hurt, tired, or anything but the king of that cage.

This I refer to as: "neutral face."

There isn't a single practice where I don't yell out, while coaching our players, "Neutral face, neutral face! Don't show it!" I burn it into my athletes' memory banks.

Don't ever show you're tired, or frazzled, or overwhelmed. As soon as the person you're up against sees even the smallest tell from you, he's going to be able to capitalize on that. Randy was badass enough to take it one step further and throw in the wink, but a good, stoic, neutral face will work wonders.

I also don't allow our hands to rest on our hips. This is part of the "neutral face" strategy. I drill this into our athletes, until it becomes second nature. By putting your hands on your hips for a breather, you're showing your opponent and everyone else that you're tired, that you're winded, that you're not 100 percent.

I've had some people who are first learning the mindset push back on this. They'll say, "Yeah, but it shows how hard you're working."

No. You don't want to show ANYTHING.

The flip side to this logic is to look for what your opponents are showing *you*. For the NFL players we train, this means looking across the field and identifying who is gasping for air. Looking for who is using the oxygen tank on the sidelines. Looking for who signed up to play a game, not to fight a war. Then targeting those weak links.

As your opponent's fatigue grows, and their body language shows it, sharpen your weapons even more. Ramp that pace up yet again.

Get in their head, show them with your attitude: Hey, getting tired, huh? Fuck, man, you're huffing and puffing over there. Huh, me? Nah, I'm not tired. I can do this shit all day long.

Get them thinking: How is he fucking smiling right now? Why the fuck is he not tired? This shit ain't fun. What's he grinning about?

One day I was at Unbreakable and brought in former Giants center Shaun O'Hara to work with our offensive linemen. When he heard me preaching the gospel of "neutral face" O'Hara let us in on a little secret I'd never known. He said his Giants' team, in the postseason one year, shifted the position of their huddle, so they could see which players on their opponent's defense had their hands on their hips and were taking in deep gasps of air . . . and how they went directly after those players. His words were music to my ears. Oh, and by the way, O'Hara's Giants won the Super Bowl that year.

Conversely, I can control my fatigue with my body language as well. Yes, I actually control how tired I am, using the magical gift God blessed us all with, between our ears.

How? Here's one example I coach into all members of Unbreakable (not just our athletes) using this simple but memorable advice: "Remember when you were a kid, playing tag or another game with your friends, or brother, or sister, and you'd fall down on the ground, totally exhausted? And they'd run up to you, twang you, and run away? What did you do? You jumped up, ran after them . . . And all of a sudden you forgot you were tired."

Fatigue can be controlled. Get your opponents to question their own hearts, not yours. As I see their wheels turning and their hands on hips, I literally get excited, and then another magical thing happens. I get so jazzed up about this, I actually forget my own exhaustion. This shift in the way I carry myself allows me to conquer that fatigue.

Use this on the field, in the cage, on the basketball court, in the hockey rink . . . in life! Use this in business. How? There's going to be conflict in every business, and that's where neutral face comes in. You can't let on that someone, or a situation, is getting to you. You want to show you're unflappable, that nothing anyone else says or does is going to affect you or how you accomplish your work. So, maintain that neutral face, keep pressing forward, until the competition starts to break . . . and you finally push it to go your way.

And when you add neutral face to the final pillar of the Unbreakable Mindset, the magic immediately becomes clearer.

PILLAR V: IT'S YOUR HONOR TO FIGHT HURT.

For this last pillar, I will let Ronde Barber lead the way.

When Ronde retired from a sixteen-year NFL career, he had the longest active-consecutive-games-played streak of any player in the NFL. A stunning 224 consecutive starts. Now mind you, he's only five-eight, 180 pounds. There were plenty of times he got CRUSHED by players who were much bigger and heavier than him. But he had one thing they didn't have: a failsafe mantra: "IT IS MY HONOR TO PLAY HURT."

He won a Super Bowl with the Buccaneers, played in five Pro Bowls, was part of the NFL All Decade Team for the 2000s, but do you want to know what he's most proud of? What's he bragged about the most? It's those 224 starts despite . . . you ready for this . . . ?

Broken forearm

Torn PCL (posterior cruciate ligament)

Broken thumb (both this and his PCL in the year he won the Super Bowl)

Bone chips in his elbow that required surgery to remove

High ankle sprain (usually a four-week injury for just about every other player)

Injured hamstring and injured quad, his first year starting

Dislocated shoulder

In Ronde's mind, these injuries made him so much more badass when he picked off an opponent's pass, despite a torn knee, a dislocated shoulder, and a sprained ankle. His idea of being gangster was to blitz off the edge and sack a much bigger quarterback with a plate inserted in his forearm or with a pulled hamstring.

"It's my honor to play hurt," he said.

I flipped the first time I heard that. It sounded like a line out of a movie. *Yes!* I decided from that day forward, I would make it my mantra too: "It's my honor to fight hurt. It's my honor to train hurt."

I can even expand this mantra and look at life through the lens of my mental health struggles, "It's my honor to LIVE hurt."

I heard an almost identical mantra from Couture toward the end of his career as well. Ronde and Randy, names separated by two letters, with hearts that are pretty damn similar.

Check it out: Randy's old ass was the heavyweight champion of the world when he was forty-four years old. At this point, he had no business fighting at heavyweight, due to his lack of size and his age, but here he was, a reigning king after having just beaten the dog shit out of six-nine Tim Sylvia, and then defending his title against 250-pound Gabriel Gonzaga, with a broken arm. Gonzaga broke Randy's arm completely in half and, instead of wincing, Randy said to himself, "The ref and doctor will stop this fight if we complete the round, so, I better finish him off before that."

Couture, broken arm and all, picked up the much-larger Gonzaga, flipped him over, slammed him on his nose, broke it, and rained down punches, until the fight was called.

However, that's not the story I am getting at to highlight his honor in fighting hurt.

Randy's next title defense was against Brock Lesnar. Brock walks around at about 300 pounds. He is an absolute monster. You may know him from WWE, but he's also one of the best college heavyweights in the history of college wrestling. His wrestling is very, very real!

What nobody knows, however, probably not even Brock, is that Randy burst the bursa sac in his elbow a couple of weeks before the fight and was unable to lift any weights. He couldn't really train the way he wanted, and he had a hard time even straightening his arm.

Leading up to the fight, I made the mistake of saying to Randy, "RC, why don't we pull out of this until you're healthy? You should be 100 percent against this guy."

Seems logical, doesn't it?

"Pull out of the fight?!?!" he yelled at me. "I'm not pulling out of the fight. Can you imagine if I can beat him, and I'm only at 50 percent? Even if I just slam him at 50 percent? That's what I care about. Think about what that says. That's my honor! I'm not pulling out of this fight. Don't even bring it up again!"

Whoaaaaaa, settle down there, sheriff. It's one of the rare times Randy has jumped my shit in our twenty years of friendship.

By the way, Randy nearly got his wish in the fight. He dropped down, grabbed a hold of the massive legs of Lesnar, lifted him up for what was going to be a slam. Right as Randy was about to put him up and over, Lesnar grabbed the cage in what was a clear violation of the rules. Nevertheless, it stopped Couture from lifting and slamming him. That was Randy's window, injured elbow and all. That was his shot. In the next round, Lesnar clipped Randy with a punch behind the ear, to take the title from him, and with it, the UFC Heavyweight Championship belt. It would be the last night Couture wore gold around his waist. He had that much at stake, yet he still walked into battle, injured, knowing he could lose championship status forever.

Fights come and go. What makes Randy the kind of badass that I'm honored to call my friend, and to train the next generation of fighters with, is that gangster mindset he carries with him, always, despite the outcome of any one fight.

You can bet your ass that Randy, and Tony, and Ronde weren't worried about how they were going to look, or what people were going to think. No, they were too busy focusing on what they could do with what they had in the moment. That's how you want to live your life—focused on yourself, on what you're getting out of the fight, on what you can learn. You want to grow and emerge even more badass the next time out.

What happens should you lose? You learn, that's what you do. Every loss presents an opportunity to improve, presents an opportunity to overcome. Adversity is a gift. It's how we grow. But in order to truly do this, we need to take our ego and pride out of it. Being Unbreakable means we have been knocked down, we have taken losses, we have been hurt, but we got back up every single time.

When you worry about what the rest of the world thinks, you actively hold yourself back from your potential. You put your focus where it's useless to be, on how you're going to appear to other people, which doesn't allow you to go a hundred percent. Anyone who's ever really fucking tried doesn't go around laughing at people.

A lot of times, when you're being unrelenting, and you're fighting hurt, and you're pushing past your breaking point, you look like shit. Who cares? That's one of the reasons we don't have mirrors at Unbreakable. Yep, you read that right. We're the only gym in America with zero mirrors. Why? I don't want anybody's backs to their teammates because they're looking at themselves in the mirror. We are in this together. But I also want us to be able to fail over and over and over again. Failing and learning from those fails makes us stronger.

For me, I just GO, and I don't really care how it looks. This is applicable in all areas of life! I'll deal with the embarrassment afterward, if I have to. I mean, you're gonna be embarrassed sometimes, one way or the other, right? Might as well go for it.

You've seen how these five pillars work, how they separate good players from great players and great players from legends. Now it's your turn, teammate. Learn 'em, apply 'em, perfect 'em:

- Find out who the best is . . . and do more than them.
- Be relentless.

- Push your breaking point, push your breaking point, push your breaking point.
- Neutral face: don't ever show you're hurt or tired.
- It's your honor to fight hurt.

If you combine all five of these pillars of the Unbreakable Mindset, think of the success you can have in so many different areas of your life. It can happen for anybody. It can happen for you, teammate. I need you to believe, you deserve to believe. You can change your life TODAY.

But, always, do all of this while being true to yourself. Be . . . well, that leads us to our next chapter and the lesson it contains.

TEAMMATE LET ME ASK YOU:

How do you talk to yourself? If you're like me and the roommates in your head are assholes, probably not very nicely. I get it. Breaking lifetime patterns is no joke. But let's start small, like I would do on the first day someone comes into Unbreakable. More important than training your muscles is the work we do on what's between your ears. Tell yourself: *I am relentless. I am Unbreakable. No matter how much I'm hurting or struggling right now, I'm not going to show it on my face. I'm not going to give up. I'm going to push harder!* BECAUSE YOU ARE WHAT YOU PUT IN, NOT THE RESULTS THAT COME OUT.

BE AUTHENTIC
(AKA HOW I LANDED THE
SPYGATE SCOOP)

Look, we couldn't end this book without getting into the one story I know all football fans really want to hear.

Yes, Spygate.

So, this is the definitive account of the bombshell that was Spygate and . . . how it taught me a major lesson about success in *all* areas of life, which now I'm teaching you, teammate.

Picture this. It was November 2007, and I was at one of my favorite beaches in the US, Kiawah Island, South Carolina, where my family was celebrating Thanksgiving, when my phone rang:

"Can you please hold for Senator Specter?" a polite voice asked me.

"Sure, I can," I answered, already grinning. "Sure, I can." I turned to my dad, Ed, who was standing next to me. "Arlen Specter is calling me," I said, trying to act all sorts of professional but also thinking, *You've got to be shitting me.*

"Really, Arlen Specter?" my dad asked. Even for someone

like me, who has a Forest Gump–like knack for getting in the middle of things, this was a stretch. The senator from Pennsylvania had had a long, distinguished career, which he'd kicked off by investigating JFK's assassination. I mean: Kennedy . . . Glazer, hmmmm, which of these names doesn't belong, and why? Specter was once named by *TIME* magazine as one of our nation's ten best senators. And now, here he was, calling me. Kind of a step down for him, I would think.

A few months earlier, in September 2007, I had scored the biggest scoop in NFL history! That's not an exaggeration; it was, and still remains, the biggest scoop of all time in the world of NFL reporting. I'd gotten my hands on the only existing copy of the Spygate tape, the video showing the Patriots cheating against the Jets by illegally videotaping their defensive coaches' signals. It was so big, NFL commissioner Roger Goodell fined the Patriots Organization $250,000, head coach Bill Belichick an additional $500,000, and stripped them of a first-round draft pick (which would have been the thirty-first pick of the 2008 draft). All the other video tapes had been destroyed by the NFL. This was the only one remaining.

Let me set the stage. The tape first came into my possession on a Wednesday. I planned to break the story and air the tape on our next *FOX NFL Sunday*, which was, obviously, on a Sunday. Four days may seem like no big thing. But as a reporter, hoping that nobody else would suddenly, somehow, get their hands on the tape and release it before I could—that wait was absolutely excruciating. Oh, and no, I won't say how I got it, who I got it from, or anything else that can leave clues here, because there was a $1 million fine for anyone who was found to give out such inside information. Can you imagine that? A million dollars!

When I first got the tape, I popped it into my TV, and there on my screen was a whole bunch of . . . tits and ass? *What the fuck?* All that I saw was some asshole behind the camera, zooming into girls' boobs, then, to fans sitting in the crowd, and then, back to the boobs and asses of the Jets cheerleaders/dance crew. I was sure my source had totally played a joke on me, which I would have deserved due to the countless jokes I have played on my friends. Still, I couldn't *not* keep watching, just in case. The video continued, only to reveal . . . more T&A. Air was totally deflated out of my emotional tires. And then, suddenly, Tom Brady, throwing warm-up passes, came into frame. Then . . . more T&A.

I was absolutely gutted. You don't understand, this was going to be my second ever week in studio at FOX. SECOND!! Howie Long, Terry Bradshaw, and Jimmy Johnson had been together for the show's, at that point, first *fifteen years* of existence. The last thing they wanted was some new dude they didn't really know on their playground. And here I'd thought this video would be my "in" with them, my chance to prove I belonged.

Here I'd had dreams of walking in, my second week, with the biggest "get" of all time, and instead I'm watching freaking Girls Gone Wild: New England Patriots Edition. Not only that, but that same week my marriage had fully dissolved. It hadn't been good for a while, but I'd held out hope that it could be salvaged. And that week, of all weeks, was when it had completely crumbled into a big smoking pile of divorce. Two kicks right in my life's nuts. I sat there watching the video and thinking, *My life is so incredibly shitty right now I'm about to . . . whoa, whoa whoaaaaaa. . . . what did the screen just change to?*

OH . . . MY . . . GOD!!! More like, THANK YOU MY BEST FRIEND GOD!!!

This was not a prank, this was not bogus, this was my golden Wonka ticket. *Holy shnikees.*

Suddenly, there on the screen was exactly what the Patriots and Bill Belichick had been accused of doing, during a September 9 game against the Jets. The camera zoomed in on the Jets' defensive coaches, recording the hand signals they used to call plays into the linebacker on the field, who would then bark them out to the rest of his teammates. The video then shot up to show the scoreboard, which kept track of the current play's down, distance, and time on the clock. And then, the play would be run. Rinse, repeat, and over and over again. Every Jets' signal was being stored on video.

The advantage of taping opponents was that the Patriots could then have had someone log and study that information. The next time they played that opponent, they could watch their coaches for those same hand signals in similar situations. And then, they could radio down to the Patriots coaches, who would warn quarterback Tom Brady, via the speaker in his helmet, to watch out for certain blitzes, coverages, schemes. I have to be honest: as I watched the tape and digested its full implications, I found it pretty damn brilliant. Brilliant but illegal. Very illegal by league rules.

So here I was, with the NFL's version of the Zapruder film (the film showing the JFK assassination). I'll admit, if anything could have helped me to feel more confident about my role at FOX and heal my broken heart, this was it. I was still hurting, but this was the holy grail of scoops, and better than all the boosts any marriage counselor could have given me.

The previous week, I'd had one segment, but David Hill, chairman of our network, had decided he wanted to spread me out across the show, because fans were starting to really crave inside information. It was 2007, the start of what would become a boom in insiders on cable and network sports shows.

Early Sunday morning, about three hours before our show was to air, our producer at the time, Scott Ackerson (we now have our guy Bill Richards in that role), stood in front of the room during our production meeting and kicked it off with, "Before we start, one change we are making: Jay isn't going to have one segment anymore. He's going to have three. But today, he is going to have four, so you are going to lose a little time elsewhere."

Well shit, Scotty, don't say it like THAT!

"He's having a fourth segment because . . ." Scotty paused. "He got the video."

Total stunned silence. Usually, we are listening but often whispering our own little side conversations and jokes. But now . . . silence. Until Howie popped out of his chair. "You're telling me, he has the video?" he yelled, with a few veins starting to bulge out of his neck, never looking at me.

"Yes," said Scotty.

"The actual video!?" Howie barked again, even stronger this time.

"Yes!" Scotty said.

Hall of Fame coach Jimmy Johnson, sitting across the room from me, caught my eye.

"Do you really have it?"

"Yeah, I actually really do," I said, shaking my head, as amazed as they were.

The confusion in the room had its own weather pattern, and it was about to boil over. But suddenly, Bradshaw let out the most incredibly welcomed whistle I have ever heard in my life. *Phewwwweeep!* "Welp, he's okay with me!" he said.

With that whistle, my sadness over my marriage ending washed away, and along with it, my fear of never being let into the *FOX NFL Sunday* fraternity.

Fifteen minutes before I went on FOX to actually break the story of the tape, I called NFL commissioner Roger Goodell on his cell phone. He didn't answer. So, I texted him something along the lines of: *Dude, call me real quick. Important, I got some shit.* (Yes, that's the actual way I text the commissioner of the NFL. I am the same with everyone. I've always texted that way to my grandmother, head coaches, players, team owners, my friends, my rabbi, shit, even governors I know . . . everyone.) Love me or hate me, at least you know what you're getting, I think there is tremendous value in being authentic.

A couple of minutes later, Roger called back.

"I have the Spygate video," I said.

He was totally calm, which surprised me. Completely calm but confused. "How can you have the tape? We destroyed them."

"All but one I guess," I said.

And then came the real shock: "Well, good get on your end. That's pretty big," he said.

It took me by surprise, but I didn't have time to process all of that, because I needed to quickly try to plant one seed.

"I know you're going to want to launch an investigation, but Roger, I am asking you not to," I said.

"Jay, how can I not?"

"Roger, I am asking you not to, because I am going to drop so many false tips, and lead people down so many false roads, in order to protect my own sources. Many, many others will seem guilty, and that will just shatter trust in the league office and mess with too many people."

"I hear ya."

And that was that. He hung up, and I rushed back into our Avocado Room to prepare for my broadcast.

Three hours later, my life would change forever. I went from an NFL Insider to a major topic on late-night talk shows and most of the radio shows in America. It was so incredibly bizarre, watching a show that highlighted my story, or listening to them try to uncover who my sources were. For those ensuing months I felt like I was a central figure in an espionage thriller instead of an NFL reporter.

Commissioner Goodell, of course, launched a massive investigation. The NFL went through phone records, brought people in for interviews, re-interviewed people, made a ton of calls to seek my sources. It was bananas. The NFL never found them, though. They may think they know who it is, but trust me on this, they never, ever, ever, even got close to her, or him, or them. Never even close. The actual way I got the video, well, that will have to be in the book I write thirty years from now, provided my sources give me the all-clear.

The day we aired the actual Spygate video footage on *FOX NFL Sunday*, countless other reporters suddenly launched their own stories, trying to break the story of "Who gave Glazer the tape?"

Add to this the fact that Arlen Specter was now calling me on my cell phone, and this entire affair felt more like real-life spy stuff, not just spying in the NFL.

Oh, and before I get back to my call with Specter, I might as well confess that when the NFL did their own investigation into my source, I may have, kind of, sort of, laid some breadcrumbs down a false path, toward a completely different person. Possibly. Might have. Okay, fuck it, yeah, I did.

All this is to say that the investigation had been extremely hairy there for a couple of months. By Thanksgiving, it had started to die out some . . . and then Congress called.

"Jay, great work on Spygate," Senator Specter said. I knew his office had been trying to set up a call. But I'd been having the best couple of months of my professional life. I was a little busy. I know that sounds pretty stupid on my end. Actually, as I sit here, writing that sentence, it fully dawns on me, *Did I really big-time the senator because of scheduling conflicts?* More than a few times in my life I have, not so rhetorically asked myself, *What the fuck is wrong with you Glazer?!?* This would be one of those moments. *What the fuck IS wrong with you Glazer?* I think Senator Specter was about to ask himself that same question.

"We'd love that copy of the tape you have," Specter continued. "Now, Jay, if you give me your copy of Spygate, I will TRADE you the biggest scoop you've ever had in your life."

Hmmm, a trade. Love the subterfuge.

"What you got?" I asked, trying not to laugh because I knew it was absolute bullshit from the start.

"Oh, I can't tell you until you give me the tape, but it'll be bigger than Spygate," the senator said.

Oh, okay, sure I'll give you the only known existent copy of the videotape just because you told me you'd give me something better in exchange. Sure. Wow, what can go wrong with this deal?

"What could be bigger than Spygate?" I said, squishing my toes into the sand. I was about as relaxed as I ever get. I work well in chaos, as opposed to in normalcy or calmness. This is one of the ways, I have learned, those battles against the gray probably help me. I have chaos going on inside my head most of the time, because of my depression and anxiety, so when it happens in real time, I'm already used to it.

"Trust me on this, you've just got to give me your copy first, and I'll give you something that's even bigger."

I'd enjoyed our verbal sparring for long enough. I was, for once, going to get serious and very deliberate in how I answered him back. Regardless of how dumb his approach in his current negotiation was, he was still a US senator, and Arlen Specter at that.

"Senator Specter, respectfully, I just hit a grand slam in the bottom of the ninth, with two outs, to beat the Yankees in the World Series," I said. "I don't know what you could possibly give me that's bigger than this tape. I'm Bobby Thomson right now." I know, I know. Thomson beat the Brooklyn Dodgers in the bottom of the ninth with a home run, not the Yankees, but you get the point.

"Well, Jay—" he said.

Meanwhile, my dad was watching me closely—I was really talking to Senator Arlen Specter. Maybe for me this was normal, but this was not normal by any *normal* standards.

"Respectfully, Mr. Specter," I said. I'm never one to miss an opportunity. So now that he'd gotten me on the phone, I had some thoughts for him. "I don't think this is where our tax dollars should be going. We're just sports. We're just escapism. There's so much more for the government to be dealing with than me and my copy of Spygate, which is something that's already been handled."

"Well, Jay," he continued. Something in his voice had shifted—I'd been breaking stories long enough to know a thing or two about people—and I could tell he was getting ready to bring it home, big time. "I didn't want to resort to this, but I'm just going to tell you, if you don't give me what I'm requesting, then you could be facing jail time for obstruction of justice."

Jail time? Did he just say jail time? Well, that's a bit extreme, no? I'd expected some sort of curveball, but I didn't think he would have the nuts to threaten me with actual jail time. Can you imagine what that scene at Rikers Island would be like? A gang of hardcore murderers come check out the new guy: "What you in here for, boy?"

"Ummmmm, I'm here because of the Patriots."

"Whoaaaa, nobody fuck with the new guy!"

But seriously? Jail time? This threat, bizarre as it was, demanded an even more bizarre response. "Jail time?" I said. "What the hell do I care? All I do is fight and lift anyway."

It wasn't like this was even the first time I'd been threatened with jail time for refusing to reveal my source. Former Raiders team president, Bruce Allen, had said publicly that I should be put in front of the federal grand jury to reveal my sources when, in 2002, I broke the story of the infamous BALCO steroid scandal infiltrating the NFL. I had an extremely angry encounter with Allen as a result of it and told him, point-blank, I was so pissed about his trying to sully my name because of how proud I am of my accuracy in reporting that the next time I saw him, I was going to . . . "Beat your fucking ass!" Yes, I said this to the president of the Raiders. I was fucking pissed. To his credit, Allen said, "You are THAT mad? Oh, we need to fix this. Can I come in and take you out to dinner and hash this out?" Good to his word, he came to NYC and, yes, we went to dinner, and I told him how and why this angered me so much. My accuracy, to me, was the one thing nobody can ever take away from me, and he was trying to do exactly that.

Herein lies the ultimate lesson of this chapter, which we'll touch on more in a bit. Be authentic. Too many of us try to be something we are not or try to act a certain way to impress others. That's when we get into trouble, teammate. Just be authentic. We all have things that make us different, so learn to lean on what makes you, well, YOU. And then run with it.

I know what my limitations are. I know what my struggles are, but I also know what I'm good with. I know I can find solutions when the shit is flying. I can coach others to truly believe in themselves. I am a badass but vulnerable communicator. I am loyal as fuck. I know I have trust and my work ethic is incredibly intense. So, I always try to work on where I struggle, and these qualities in my life that I'm good at, I viciously protect them.

Oh, and back to being a little too authentic with the senator from Pennsylvania. I should have thought this whole jail thing through more thoroughly by then.

"What are you doing?" my dad said, panicked. I might have been relaxed, but he was understandably worried. I held my hand up to him, indicating I had it handled.

Senator Specter and I had nothing more to say to each other, and so I got off the phone, careful not to make any promises or to open my mouth any wider than I already had. As you're probably starting to glean, this is not an easy job for me.

"What are you doing?!" my dad repeated.

"Trying to show them that I'm off," I said.

"You're trying to what?"

Off, ya know, too crazy to reason with.

Hey, it made sense to me. Then, I called people at FOX to tell them what had happened. Here I was, the C-minus student who'd gotten the biggest scoop, ever, in NFL history, a scoop that had now launched two investigations—one by the NFL, one by Congress.

"You're trying to show them that you're off?" Asked Rick

Jaffe, my producer during the week at FOX and editor of Fox Sports.com.

"Yeah, trying to show them that I'm off."

"Trying to show the Senate that you're off?"

Geesh, Rick, way to sound like my dad.

Hey, it seemed like a pretty damn good plan to me. I soon got proof that I was right about the merits of my approach. The next time I was at FOX, some of my bosses there, including George Greenberg and David Hill, laid out what I should do next. "We're now telling you—shut the fuck up," they said, though I do think they were laughing at the absurdity of it all.

"I'm trying to show them I'm off," I continued, sticking to my plan.

"You're trying to show Congress that you're off? Think how ridiculously stupid that is."

"Look, it's happening with you guys right now," I said, proving my point. "You guys are throwing your hands up in the air. You can't deal with it."

Here I was, totally down on myself, in the tank, over a failed marriage, and a new a gig where I felt nobody wanted me. I had zero stability in my life. I felt like the sky was falling. And then, *BOOM*, just like that, what came the day after next Tuesday changed my life forever. But really, it wasn't just the Spygate scoop that turned everything around. It was how I handled it—it was me, being my usual authentic, "did he really just say that?" self that caused the outcome to be a positive that would ripple out in my life for years . . . is still rippling out to this day. Same Jay Glazer, on both days, in both moments. And it was the fact that I didn't allow myself to be warped, or changed, because I felt the pressure to do so, to try to save my marriage, to fit in at work, that actually helped me to build the one and only life of my choosing.

What I'm saying is that positive change happened because I was authentic. I have had a career of huge scoops, all from relationships, because I was authentic. Every single one of them. That *Ballers* role? Me, being authentic. How I coach people . . . with pure authenticity!

I know, this may be uncomfortable or scary for some of you. Maybe I do have the advantage, after all, because I already feel like the sky is falling on a "good" day, so I might as well just be myself, consequences be damned. At least then I get the rush of knowing I was true to myself and true to what I value—my reputation for integrity, those relationships I've worked so hard to build, being someone who's not afraid to speak the truth as I see it.

Your own version of authenticity will look and feel different, teammate. It might not come as naturally to you as it does to me. But good news! Like everything else in life, it can be practiced and learned. Start small. Stand up for yourself, or what you believe in. Say what you're really thinking, even when everyone else is just going along. The rewards will be just as huge for you as they were for me. Perhaps even better, you'll start attracting other authentic people, and those are the teammates you want to keep for life!

My life is crazy because I'm crazy, which is why I attract so much other craziness. These days I'm trying to be authentic about learning to love myself, hoping to attract more of that in my life. If you are loving, and stay authentic, you will attract other loving people. If you are an asshole and stay authentic, you'll probably attract other assholes. These days, I'd rather attract the former than the latter in my life.

Which brings us to the home stretch. Ahhh, yes, my life. A life that I am using now to help so many others, but a life that I was pretty close to losing, not that long ago.

TEAMMATE, LET ME ASK YOU:

What makes you authentically you? I'm not just requesting the highlights reel you'd give at a job interview. I'm talking about AUTHENTICITY, what you and you alone possess. Dig deep and list where you struggle and what you're good with. Challenge yourself to find a moment in the next week when you vow to be more you (hopefully the loving you, not the asshole you)—be vulnerable, stand up for yourself, speak your mind, crack that joke. Are you scared? Good! BECAUSE THAT MEANS THE REAL YOU IS REALLY LIVING.

12

BE PROUD OF
YOUR SCARS

Mr. Couture, can you please tell Mr. Glazer to put his phone down? This is a very, VERY serious situation," The nurse from Cedars-Sinai Hospital in Los Angeles pleaded with Randy Couture.

Couture, who you've met by now in the pages of this book, wasn't making much headway in this fight against me. Trying to convince me to put my phone down . . . zero shot, Randy.

I had just come out of what was supposed to be an easy-peasy procedure on my spine. Instead, I was in serious physical distress. Only, I didn't have time to be this out of it right now . . . because this also happened to be the day NFL free agency began for the 2014 season.

"Bud, I think you need to listen to these nurses. I think this is real," Randy said, much less aggressively than he talks to me after he slams me in training.

"Dude, I don't even fully understand what the fuck is happening right now and it's the start of free agency. I gotta be on my phone when everyone in the league calls."

"I think this is beyond that, brother," he responded.

If there is anyone who knows how to handle me, it's him. He is the nicest human being on the face of the planet, anywhere on the planet, outside of a cage or a wrestling mat that is. Once he steps into the cage, he's the most sadistic asshole on the planet . . . and that's to his best friends; forget his opponents! So, when I'd gone into Cedars early that morning for a simple clean-up, of a disc that ruptured AGAIN, my third rupture at the time of my L4, L5 disc (I am now up to four), I had Mr. Expendable as my emergency contact, in case anything went wrong.

A lot went wrong. Really, really wrong.

I fully came to, lying on a gurney, and Randy was who I saw. That's how I knew I was still alive, because if it was heaven, it wouldn't be his ugly-ass mug that I opened my eyes to . . . unless God decided to play a joke on me for all the jokes I've played on others. I was on that gurney in the critical care area of the hospital, IV line needled into my left arm, breathing tube in my nose, all sorts of shit getting pumped into me in an attempt to keep me alive. Still did not understand what had happened, but I knew I didn't have time for it. This shit was definitely not fitting into my schedule.

Despite my situation, teams and players were calling, either giving me scoopage on a major free agency signing, needing my help to convince a team that a certain player was worth their courtship, or asking me if a certain team would fit a player's personality. In the high-pressure game of inside NFL scoop reporting, I couldn't let a little thing like death get in the way, right?

But for the first time in as many seasons as I could remember, I didn't break a handful of scoops that day. I didn't break a single one. Instead, something much bigger than getting a scoop happened. That was the day that would launch me to find my bigger purpose, to help improve the world. That was the day that would change the course my life, and as I now know, so many other lives. But in order for all of that to happen, I first needed to stay alive.

Oh, and how did I find myself in this position in the first place?

The night before this "routine" procedure, my friend Craig Ley and I went out to a very early dinner. I needed to stop eating twelve hours before I was due to get anesthesia, so the food could fully digest. Right after the meal, both Craig and I felt some indigestion. But I didn't have another thought about it, went to bed, woke up at six a.m. for the procedure.

Pieces of my discs had ruptured and sat on the nerve, causing major inflammation and pain. This procedure at Cedars was pretty routine, and in my fucked-up mind, Couture and I would be training later that day. For those with back pain, you know what I'm describing . . . holy shit it's terrible, but when they alleviate that nerve pain, oh my goodness, there's nothing like that feeling of relief.

A few years earlier, when I'd gotten my back cleaned up, I lied to my doctors and told them my ride was picking me up downstairs. They walked me outside, and I actually strolled down the street to the Beverly Wilshire Hotel (the hotel in the movie *Pretty Woman*) for a burger and a beer. I threw myself a "pain free" party at ten a.m., by myself. "Glazer, party of one, Glazer, party of one fucked-up individual."

This time, however, was very different. For this procedure when they put me under and placed me on my stomach, with my face set down into a face cradle, I threw up the entire meal from the night before, which apparently, had never fully digested, along with stomach acid and bile, and I . . . drowned in it. Yup, I drowned in it.

I'm not sure what happened exactly, because I was not awake for any of this, but I was told that I threw up profusely, to the point where it came out of the face cradle (which for some reason was more of a bowl with no drainage), overflowing on both sides. At the same time, it poured down my esophagus and filled my lungs, immediately burning and infecting them both. According to what the doctor and nurses told me, days later, after I drowned in this shit, I began convulsing on the table. The doctor quickly flipped me over to shove a tube down my throat to suction out the vomit.

Stomach acid on lung tissue is a horrible, often fatal combination.

Upon reviving me, the nurses and doctor immediately put me in a wheelchair, strapped an oxygen mask to my face, and whisked me up to the head of respiratory at Cedars-Sinai. I still didn't understand what was going on. I do remember feeling like I was freezing, and I just wanted to shut my eyes and go back to sleep. This caused more panic.

"Try to stay awake!" the doctors and nurses ordered me, continuously. "Mr. Glazer, you need to keep your eyes open. You need to keep your eyes open and stay with us."

Stay with us? Why can't I just go to sleep, sleep it off?

As the doctors later told me, I had double aspiration pneumonia. Often, when people die of a drug overdose, it's because their lungs aspirated, or they inhaled vomit into their lungs, and having those toxins in their lungs leads to death. Unfortunately, for me, the acid and bile went into both of my lungs. Your trachea has a valve that is intended to prevent this from happening. Only, mine didn't work. I guess I have to be different

at everything, even when I don't want to be. This time was supposed to be no different than the other three clean-ups I'd
had . . . except it was. Very different.

Back to the gurney. The nurses moved me over to critical
care, where I was to be watched over, twenty-four/seven, so I
didn't, ya know . . . die. My oxygen levels were in the 82–84 percent range when they brought me in, and my heart rate was in
the 130s, because it was trying to overcompensate for my lungs
being burned and not working right. Proper oxygen level is 98–
100 percent. Sooooo, mine was . . . not good.

The beeps of my heart rate monitor were raging. The nurses
stuck another IV in me, snapped another breathing mask over
my face, with vaporized medication to go down into my lungs,
and put a tube in my nose for oxygen. They were working hard
to save me, when all of the sudden I realized, *Oh shit, I gotta
work, too.*

I'm not sure how I had my phone on me, but I'd come to
enough to realize that it was blowing up with NFL calls. Picture
this scene: I pulled my cell phone from my gown, somehow, and
like it was any other workday, I started texting teams back, who
were asking me if certain players would be a fit for them.

A FaceTime call came in from Lovie Smith, head coach of
the Buccaneers, and I answered, the breathing mask still on my
face, looking like Bane from Batman. Lovie started telling me
they were reversing course on signing a certain free agent. As
Lovie was speaking, he turned to look into his phone for the
first time, and well, he reacted as if he saw a ghost, or someone
who was minutes away from becoming one.

"What happened, big guy?" he asked.

"Lovie, I'm not really sure. They say I have double aspiration
pneumonia, but I haven't been feeling sick at all. I don't under-

stand really, and I'm trying to work, but they got all these tubes and masks and shit on me. I just wanna work."

"Jay, you need to sit this one out. We will all still be here, big guy. We need you healthy. Sammy needs you healthy."

My response? Even when he invoked my son, Sammy, who I love more than anything? "I hear ya, I got the Eagles calling on the other line."

I spoke with the Eagles, then the Bears, then the Seahawks, then players who were suddenly in a free agent frenzy. All the while, the nurses were monitoring the blaring symphony of my beeping heart rate and dropping oxygen, asking me to please, for goodness sakes, *get off the phone.*

Soon, Jared Allen, who was a free agent, FaceTimed me to discuss a few of his options. He had the same reaction as Lovie. "What the . . . dude, what happened?" he asked, his shock blazing across his face.

That's when Couture walked back into the room. Apparently, he'd left when I was too out of it to notice. The medical staff pleaded with him again, asking if he could talk some sense into me. He tried, but I kept answering my phone. As more teams called, word about my condition started to spread around the league. Suddenly, TMZ posted an article that said I was fighting for my life. It was absolute chaos. Beeps from the machines, our phones buzzing like crazy, nurses frantically working on and around me.

Couture, who like me is great in chaos, was once again, at the imploring of the nurses, trying to talk me into giving it all a rest. But even he eventually turned to the nurses in defeat. "Yeah, he's probably not going to listen to us," Couture said. He walked back out of the room to update more concerned friends. And then . . .

. . . This is where everything changed.

My oxygen started dropping, 82, 80, 78, 76, 74 . . .

The beeps started getting louder. All of a sudden . . . how do I describe this? The best way I can say it is . . . the entire room suddenly shifted; it moved to across the room. Let me try to give you a better grip on this. It was as if I was in the room, but I saw the entire room, as it moved about ten feet away from me. I was there, but also not inside the room. I was looking at the room, but it was suddenly at the end of a short tunnel. I knew where I was, but the room was moving away from me.

Wait a minute, am I fucking dying here?! Is that what's going on?

"Mr. Glazer, please, *PLEASE* put your phone down, and relax, and breathe," a nurse said, now rather firmly.

Holy shit, that IS what's going on here.

I finally . . . put my phone down. Instead of looking down at my phone, I looked up and . . . started talking to God. Not out loud but rather from within. Then I closed my eyes to focus on my conversation. "God, I may be about to see you, but I think I have more to do in this world. If it's my time, thank you for always being there for me, I love you."

Yes, I said "I love you" to God in that moment.

"But if there is more that I am supposed to do in this world, if there is unfinished business for me . . . can you help me help myself get through this?"

A lot of people make deals with God when bad things appear imminent. We do it all the time. And then, how many of us just forget to follow through on our end of the deal after things turn around?

This wasn't one of those deals. I wasn't going to go back on my word.

"If I survive this, I will do more."

Teammate . . . this is no exaggeration. None. This is *exactly* what ensued next.

A few breaths after my conversation with God . . . *BOOM*, my oxygen jumped from 74 back to 92. It didn't gradually go back up. No, it literally went 74, *BAM*, 92. A huge sigh of relief could be heard, collective exhales from the trauma nurses circling my bed.

The room shifted back into the present. My heart rate started to stabilize. Perhaps my best friend up above had, in fact, agreed with me that there was more for me to do in this world before I left. And, like I said, that wasn't just a one-off promise for me. I've kept this vow front and center in my life ever since then.

That is what this book is for me. Part of me keeping my end of that deal.

Had I not made it through March 10, 2014, I know now that it would have affected a great many people. I would not have been here to start MVP. And I don't even want to think about where many of our combat veterans would be without MVP. I would not have been here to help people. Or even if I was, I might not have had the courage and clarity of purpose to coach others by drawing on my experiences with depression, anxiety, ADD. I might not have had the vision to see the power in living in the gray, using our scars to empower us, appreciating that it's okay to not always be okay, and it's strong to be vulnerable.

In that moment, all I knew was that I was ALIVE.

There's a lot that goes along with a near-death experience. Gratitude, of course. Fuck yeah. But there's guilt associated with it too. There's anxiety in surviving. Sounds crazy, right? I was actually depressed, more than normal, those first few weeks after I left the hospital. Hear me out. Because I stayed alive, and was able to start Merging Vets & Players, I learned a term from one of our vets who said he would have ended his life had it not been for MVP. A vet named Noel Huerta, who talked about having survivor's guilt, for surviving getting shot in the neck, when the teammates next to him, who also got shot, bled out. Noel, opening up in the first huddle of our NYC chapter, said that he'd long had "survivor's guilt." But now, because of his new purpose, through this vehicle of MVP, where he can save his brothers and sisters' lives, he was now calling it . . . "survivor's responsibility."

Let THAT one sink in! That's a term that can change the inner dialogue so many of us have in the world. Oh, by the way, Noel has thrived so much in MVP, we recently made him our chief operating officer.

Survivor's responsibility, what an incredible phrase.

I hope this book allows me to hold up my end of the deal, and to cope better with the pressure of this overtime I was given. This book is my version of survivor's responsibility. And my responsibility, my God-inspired mission, is to get us all to be PROUD of our scars, proud of the dark tunnels we have gone through only to come out on the other side.

Going into that surgery on that day back in 2014, I believed I was simply adding another scar. I didn't understand how powerful a lesson I would learn and now have the opportunity to pass on.

There are only two choices we have in life, teammate: either let your pain and scars bring you down or let them raise you up. I'm insisting that you be proud of them. Every single one of them! They make us different, and as I've realized, even more than that, they empower us! I'm talking about all kinds of scars: mental scars, emotional scars, physical scars . . . be proud of every fucking one of them. Look in that mirror every morning and love yourself up for the hard shit you've overcome to earn those scars, both inside and out. They symbolize something that tried to break us but couldn't . . . hence the name "Unbreakable."

My scars help define what I have overcome! They define me, not in a damaged way, but in an empowering way. Let your scars lift you, teammate!

A lot of my scars are emotional—between my ears, in my heart, even affecting my soul. My physical scars? Well, they are a by-product of training and fighting, which was my way of dealing with my emotional scars. Me changing the way I view my scars is as much a part of my healing as anything else.

For years and years, I ran from my scars; I hid them in shame. Too many of us try to cover up our scars, to pretend we don't have any, to look at being different as a curse. Fuck that! It's not a curse, teammate. It's a blessing. The majority of successful people dominate *because* they are different. Our scars make us different, unique. Don't hide what makes you different.

My friends who are amputees, Kirstie Ennis and Joey Jones, another badass marine in MVP who lost both his legs to an IED, they almost always wear shorts to show off their prosthetics. I think it's so brave. But do you know why they don't hide them? To allow others who have disabilities or issues to be able to approach them and learn about their struggles and their strengths. Even after losing limbs, they are using their scars to still be of service.

Thanks to all these years of MMA training, I have ruptured discs in my back seven times and have nothing left of my L4, L5. I have herniated four discs in my neck. Broken my nose SIX times and had bone cut out of there. Tore my calf. Broke my right ankle twice (I woke up during that surgery, while they were drilling . . . that was a hoot). Tore my labrum in my right shoulder. Had two rotator cuff tears, as well, in that shoulder. Dislocated my elbow. Tore a tendon on the bottom of my foot, wrestling Adrian Peterson when he was with the Saints, while I was barefoot on the turf. And partially tore my LCL.

Oh, and yes, there are the head injuries. Many, many, many of them. But other than those I've listed for you, I'm a model of stability. Proud of every single fucking one! Why? THAT IS MY ONLY CHOICE! I can't go back and fix them now, so I CHOOSE to use them to be proud. Cherish and celebrate what is unique about us, even if it's not traditionally admired.

I do not allow myself to sulk, or have a pity party, that these head injuries have likely fucked with my memory and my speech at times. I have told numerous doctors, who all want to do brain scans on me, "Don't tell me where I'm fucked up without giving me a solution." I used to do the scans then would leave depressed when they didn't have a viable cure for me. I know I'm depressed, some of which may be exacerbated by decades of getting my head smashed. I know I can't remember the names of people I've fully trained with a short time before. And I know it's because my brain doesn't send the right waves between my brain lobes anymore. I know all that, doc, you don't need to tell me about it, unless you have a solution. Because I have a solution that I think can work for us, until modern medicine catches up. My solution? Be proud of alllllll my fuckedupness . . . and the scars it has brought me. Use it as a touchstone, as strength, as a way to connect with others who are fucked up too . . . the ones who need help the most.

I spent the week after I woke up on that gurney in critical

care, most of it medically sedated, on a drug called Dilaudid, as well as an IV push of Ativan. They needed my lungs to heal. They needed me to fight back. Three days later, I again met with the head of respiratory at Cedars. This time, feeling like we were out of danger, he went into detail about what had really happened.

He told me it was one of the worst cases he'd ever seen, in which the patient survived. I threw up so much, and so much went down into my lungs, when they brought me to him, I was so far gone there was nothing they could do. All the IVs, medicines, and breathing mask were more for show. They were hoping I would believe, hoping my will would take over. It turns out, it did.

"If you were older, you would have expired," the doc very calmly explained.

Expired. I will NEVER forget that term.

"If you didn't have the inner strength, you would have died," he added. "There are two ways you can go, and you went so far over the wrong way, there was nothing we could do. But, suddenly, you jumped back over the other way."

"How?" I asked.

He kind of smirked, and didn't have a clear-cut answer, but his response took me aback.

"Do you believe in God?"

Funny, a doctor, a man of science, asking me about God? "Very much," I said.

"Well then, thank God, because we don't really have an explanation."

Science and faith can actually be friends? Wow, novel idea.

I didn't tell him about my deal with God, but it has never left my mind.

It took me another month before I was off the oxygen tank. A month! Rather than staying home and resting the way I was supposed to (common theme here is not listening to doctors) I opened Unbreakable. Yes, I opened Unbreakable while I was still using an oxygen tank on a daily basis. I would actually go scout locations, keeping the oxygen compressor in the car, to meet with realtors.

You may ask why, but I think you already know the answer. I had to open it because I now, truly, knew what Unbreakable meant. I'm so glad I didn't die that day. It's the day that gave me a different "insider" perspective that allows me to talk like this.

TEAMMATE, LET ME ASK YOU:

What makes you different? No, not the fact that you speak three languages, or you make six figures, although, sure, be proud of that too. I mean what's the part of you that maybe you're embarrassed of, or you don't normally want to talk about? The thing that, truly, is unique about you, even if you used to have it backwards and think it was ugly. What scar have you overcome? What dark tunnel have you traveled through that didn't break you? I tell this to people all the time who have beaten illnesses, addiction, or any hardships that seemed so incredibly difficult, THAT is what makes you different, and different is what leads to success. If you're beating yourself up for your struggles, stop, right now, and love yourself up for them. It's time to honor them! Seriously, BECAUSE YOU'RE DIFFERENT, MOTHERFUCKER!

13

NOW IT'S YOUR TURN, TEAMMATE

We still have a long way to go, teammate. I know, even though I've fought my way to achieve my wildest dreams, and more, there are still days I could do better. There are still people who need help. There are still pranks to be played! (Oh yeah, we're going to end on a slightly serious note here, but don't you ever, *ever* forget to laugh. It's one of the pillars of being Unbreakable! And it's one of the fiercest enemies of the gray.) But I hope that, by me writing this book, and you gleaning something from it, I'm keeping my promise to God that I made on that gurney at Cedars. It certainly feels like I am, because I can see how much my life has changed since God decided to save it. Until after the day I almost died, my two central motivators were being a great dad to Sammy and breaking scoops in the NFL. That was pretty much the extent of it. Before then, I never had that bigger purpose. I never viewed my fuckedupness as such a blessing.

Not only that, but had I not almost died that day, I would

not have made that deal. If I didn't make that deal . . . wow, there probably would be a lot of people who wouldn't be here with us today. Had I not almost died, well, a lot of lives would have been affected. I certainly wouldn't have done a deep dive into the gray, looking for ways to fight it, and then finding the words to teach these methods to you. I have my purpose now. And that means you all have someone on your team who's willing to throw his vulnerability out there on full display, to help you all deal with your anxiety, depression, and dread, or with caring about someone who's fighting the gray, or whatever you may be going through. And I'm here to inspire you to put your own vulnerability on full display. It really is our strongest muscle.

Our fight is just beginning, and truly, I need you on my team in order to wage it. Now, I understand I used a lot of big, star-fucker names to get my point across, but those were just to hold your attention, to keep you hooked on the lessons I was trying to put forth. And those big shots were in these pages because, honestly, they're members of my team who have been walking this walk with me. And I wanted to show you how much good that can do—gathering a team of your own. But big names aside, no one is as important to me as you, the person who needs this book, and who found this book, and who is going to not only learn from it, but to spread the word about it, to build our team even more.

And what are we going to tell people when we're out there waving the Unbreakable flag?! It's okay to not be okay. It's okay to live in the gray, so long as we don't let the gray win. Always, we've got to battle back against the gray, so it doesn't get too comfortable in there and think it owns us and our lives.

Are you ready to fight? You'd better be because it's time we all fought back together . . . *as one big team.* I wrote a lot in this book about finding your team. Now, you're about to go out and put these lessons to work in your own lives. But never forget that you have already found a team here with me.

I recently did a mental health talk for all of FOX Broadcast Company. There were hundreds and hundreds who watched live, and more who watched the feed after it was posted. My final message to them that day was this:

"If you see me in the hallways of FOX, and you are struggling, even if I am getting ready for a show, come over to me and tell me straight out, 'I'm struggling. I need help!' What I can promise each and every one of you is just what I tell MVP, 'I GOT YOUR BACK!'"

This is why I've been blessed to talk about fighting and football on TV, because it gives me the platform to reach so many of you, to let you know you've got a teammate who gets you, a teammate who wants to walk this walk with all of you, together. And I'll say the same thing to you that I said to my teammates at FOX. If you ever see me on the street, even if I'm with someone famous, or it looks like I'm busy, come up to me. If you need help, tell me! I will have your back, teammate.

Now, it's your turn to be there for the people in your own life. Imagine if all of you reading this book can connect, not just with me, but with each other, and become that badass team together? Use the lessons of this book and be the kind of teammates you want to have in your lives. Talk about it with others, share everything. In other words: Be of Service.

The lessons of this book aren't some big secret, or some magic trick you have to be initiated to understand. They could not be simpler. They are all right here for us to use in life. They are practical. And they are contagious if we dare to speak up and spread the word. While, yep, I said earlier how much social media fucks with our mental health, we can also use it to teach these lessons to others and to connect with our new teammates. Just like with the gray, social media doesn't have to be all bad, if we keep it in its place. That's right, use the lessons in this book to fight that fucking gray. It deserves to get its ass kicked by us!

And the greatest weapon in our arsenal?

Vulnerability is our real strength. We can't be Unbreakable without it. The only way we can kick the gray's ass is by running straight at it. A major way to do that is to TALK. Talk about everything. The more fucked up, the better. If this seems too scary, maybe do what I did earlier in this book, and make a list of all those people in your life who have stood by you, even when the gray was making you difficult to be around. And if you don't feel blessed, you've got me and our team to walk this walk with you! And if you're lucky enough to not live in the gray, is there someone you know who does? What can you do for them, TODAY, to show up?

I want you to remember one more majorly important thing, teammate. Change comes in all sorts of different packages and with varied timing. It can happen tomorrow, and that is certainly the perfect scenario, but it can also happen next week, next month. However long it takes, the key is to keep fighting, to never give up. While I want you to make the decision to change immediately, it's OK if that change doesn't happen on the spot. One thing we haven't hit on yet in this book is shame. Too often I've tried to coach people through things, and they fuck up, only to be derailed by shame. There is ZERO room for shame in my vocabulary. It doesn't exist. Many addicts fall off multiple, multiple times before they finally catch onto their path of sobriety and stick the landing. So, let's all take shame and send it off with a giant "Fuck You!" Just like we did with the gray.

Now it's time to take what you can from this book and put

it into action. Not a month from now . . . right fucking now! Go back and write down things that resonate with you. Seriously, write them down and put them next to your bed, your work computer, your fridge, wherever will help you see them each and every day, to make them part of your new routine.

Basically, I'm saying, start today, but don't expect the results right away. And don't give up, no matter how long it takes. What I ask, as you take in the lessons of this book, is try to implement them over and over and over, and be relentless in your pursuit of them, until they sink in. Be excited for change, and if you fuck up a million times along the way, I honestly don't care, nor should you. Just pick yourself up, brush yourself off, and let's walk this walk together, anew, the very next day. Oh, and when you score even the tiniest accomplishment or improvement or victory, love yourself up for it!

And don't just think of yourself as the beneficiary of these lessons. Remember, we're here to help others, teammates! What can you do right now, today, this week, to be of service to someone else? I mean the thing ONLY you can do, because of your particular talent, job, or even your fuckedupness? Or because you were tasked with it. Dig deep. It could be picking up your phone and texting a friend, just to check in. Maybe someone you know lost their job, their dad, their dog. Don't be worried that you won't find the right words. Just say hello. Maybe admit that you're struggling too. You will be letting them know they're not alone. Figure out your strengths, things you're good at, or areas you enjoy, then challenge yourself where you can be of service in those areas. And don't compare it to anyone else. Just honor yourself for doing it.

One more important note for you to keep in mind. I co-wrote this book with an absolutely amazing woman named Sarah Tomlinson. She is as much your teammate as I am. She was one of many writers I met with when I was choosing my co-writer, during three rounds of interviews that took nearly a year. However, I didn't inform her of why I chose her, over every other author, until a year or so into the process. In fact, I never told her until we reached the conclusion of our collaboration. What she didn't know was that I chose her because she, herself, is a warrior, without ever having recognized it. I chose her because she had battled cancer, and although it was a painful fight, she came through the other side of that dark tunnel, hurting, but not broken. I knew that was the kind of person I wanted on my team, to co-write this book.

Once we finished the first round of the manuscript, I finally filled her in.

"Sarah, there's something I never told you," I said as I was driving to Unbreakable one afternoon. "Do you know why I chose you over everyone else to take this journey with me?"

"Well, I know we really bonded in our interview, and I think we just hit it off, right?"

"Yes, that part is true. But I hit it off with a lot of authors. I chose you, Sarah, because you had cancer. I chose you because you beat cancer. I chose you because I wanted to see you transform from being someone who got so beat up by cancer, to someone who now knows her battle against cancer stands for something greater. If you didn't go through that dark tunnel, I wouldn't have chosen you."

Silence . . . then some tears . . . from both of us.

"So, even though it was a terrible experience for you, Sarah, your pain, well, your pain will end up helping a lot of people. I want that to fill up your soul. Sarah, you being unbreakable, and fighting back against cancer, and winning, will inspire others. THAT is why I chose you. So, I know it sucks you had to go through that, but if you hadn't, I wouldn't have chosen you. I am so glad you fought back!"

You see, no matter how bad something is, there is often something beautiful the experience is waiting to become, or a way for it to positively affect others. I am sorry you went through that, Sarah. To everyone out there who is sick, I wish it didn't have to be that way. But I don't try to figure life out. What I can say is that, just like Logan, if Sarah didn't warrior-the-fuck-up and kick cancer's ass, she would not be on this journey with us. And, yep, these were my stories, and my methods of coaching that we've been putting down on these pages. But it was Sarah's ability to connect with what I was saying, because she went through it on her own, that allowed her to be able to verbalize it in a way that will resonate, so we can help what I hope becomes millions of people.

You think in a zillion years, as she was battling for her life, she thought that one day, her battle would help save, or empower, or inspire other lives? Never once. You think while she was enduring surgeries and radiation, she would one day know the radiation would be the very thing that allowed her to help fill up others' souls? Never once. And she helped me through some dark days too.

Had Sarah not worked on this book with me, I don't know where I would be. While writing, I often had to sit in the filth and muck of the gray, intentionally. I chose not to use any of the lessons I put forth in this book, which I usually use on a daily basis, because I couldn't leave the gray. I had to lay in it so I could describe it to you, to show you all you're not alone. It got so bad during one stretch, I truly started becoming afraid that I wouldn't be able to pull myself up out of it. I've never gone through a period where I wasn't trying to get myself out of my darkness, or where I couldn't fight back against the anxiety and depression. But that's just what I did in order to write this book. Talk about fear! And talk about a time when I needed a teammate to check in on me.

Thank you, Sarah. Thank you for being the warrior you are. Thank you for helping me get through some really fucked up, dark times; thank you for helping me help others get through theirs. Thank you for being of service to me, so I can be of service to others.

See, that's what I meant earlier, about different ways of being of service to others. Sometimes it's as simple as doing a great job for someone, putting your all into something you've been tasked with. You simply never know how it can lead to something great happening for someone else who needs it. I'm sure, reading this for the first time, realizing how much she lifted me up, it has lifted Sarah through her own version of the gray.

And finally, I want to thank you, teammates. I want to thank you with all my soul. I want to thank you for saving me too. All these years, I felt I was cursed by depression, but now because I can help fight the gray—my own and others—with you, I feel for the first time in my life that God actually *blessed* me with depression.

Thank you, teammates.

ACKNOWLEDGMENTS

Thank you to all the players, coaches, GMs, executives, and anybody and everybody who has been a part of this football family for me for the last thirty years. Yes, I can't believe I'm saying that—thirty years. I'm still thinking, *Man, how did I get here?* I'm still waiting to be back in the fifth grade, and to have my mom wake me up for school and find out that none of this happened. There have been a lot of people I've been along this path with . . . people I was friends with when they were interns; and then they became head coaches, and then, they retired. So, I've been in this league for a long freaking time. And by the way, to all you guys who I've walked this walk with together over the years: I still look fantastic. You guys look like shit. Well, some of you look like shit. You guys figure out which ones.

Football, to me, is family. With that, I'd also like to say thank you to my FOX football family, Terry Bradshaw, Howie Long, Michael Strahan, Jimmy Johnson, Curt Menefee, and our producers, Bill Richards and Joel Santos. Also, thanks to the incredible people at FOX who brought me aboard and continue to lead our ship, Eric Shanks, Mark Silverman, Brad Zager, Larry Jones, and Jacob Ullman. And thanks to the past crew of David Hill, Ed Goren, George Greenberg, Scott Ackerson, and to Rick Jaffe, who was my editor at FOX when minute-by-minute breaking sports news became a thing. Thank you, also, to Don Martin and everyone at FOX Radio.

I'd like to acknowledge and thank all the people who have punched, kicked, kneed, or elbowed me in the head over the years, all those brothers of mine, literally, in arms and limbs. You have no idea how much you helped me, not hurt me: Chuck Liddell, Randy Couture, Jay Hieron, Jason Borba, all my fight teams, and the crew I've had over the years, including in the early days, Renzo Gracie, and now Royce Gracie and Mark Kerr.

Thank you to Nate Boyer and all of my MVPers—there's too many of you to name but many of you will see your names in the pages of this book. Without you all, this book would not have been possible, or meaningful. You all gave me the support and motivation to be of service to others. My life has been blessed because we've had people like you protecting us, and now, I get to call myself your brother, so thank you, all. I love you guys and gals.

Thank you to my Unbreakable family, including my long-time partner, Lindsey Berg, the Venit family, the Sullivan family, Zach, Justin, the whole coaching staff, and all our crew there.

I surround myself with a group of badass women I'm proud of like Lindsey, Kirstie Ennis, Ava Knight, Nikki Ziering, and Kami Craig. Thank-you to all of you.

I've had a lot of people who have walked this walk with me over the years. Thank you to my friends Tony Lapenna, Craig

Ley, Ben Heldfund, Scott Smith, Constance Schwartz, and Mike Morini.

Thank you to my family, my mom, dad, brother, who get pissed off that I don't visit enough, but I'm trying to help other people's families, and I hope you can understand that sacrifice and be proud of me for it.

To my son, Sammy, I never knew you could love another human being like this until I met you. Thanks for putting up with all your dad's antics. I know we've laughed a lot, we've cried, we've hugged. I hope I make you feel proud.

To my longtime agent, you're more than an agent, you're a confidante, manager, everything, Maury Gostfrand.

To my literary agents, Jan Miller, Lacy Lynch, and Dabney Rice, and everyone at Dupree Miller & Associates.

To my editor Carrie Thornton and everyone at my publisher, Dey Street, including Matthew Daddona, Liate Stehlik, Ben Steinberg, Kell Wilson, Maureen Cole, Evangelos Vasilakis, and Pam Barricklow.

Thanks to Mike Bayer for introducing me to my amazing literary team.

To my cowriter, Sarah Tomlinson, who became a pseudotherapist for me and helped lift me back up out of the gray, when I sat in it for the purposes of describing it in this book, to help others who feel it.

To my crew at GNC, Josh Burris, Rachel Jones, and Anthony Mianzo, I cannot tell you what your contributions and generosity have meant to our MVP team, thank you.

Frank Mahar and the team at Genesco, who have been so supportive over the years.

All the people at Original Footwear. Proud to walk the walk together in Altama shoes.

To DJ, Lev, and my whole *Ballers* family.

To Suzi Landolphi and the rest of my therapists, I love you and appreciate you all. Thank you for keeping the roommates in my head speaking nicely to one another (sometimes).

To Logan Nobriga, my little badass who kicked leukemia's ass, thank you for always inspiring me and helping to start a movement when you didn't really understand what your battle would turn into.

To everyone I've had these crazy, manic sessions around, and you've still remained by my side. It's hard for me to understand a lot of times, but maybe one day, with all of this together, I'll realize how special I really am, because you guys and gals are still walking this walk with me. And to everyone who's going to show me love in the future, who I just don't know about yet, I figure a preemptive thanks is appropriate.

And to all of you out there who are reading this, I've got you, I appreciate you, and I love you. To everyone else who isn't OK, thank you for bonding with me, to make sure we all know it's OK to not be OK.

And of course, to my best friend, God! Sometimes just feeling like I'm not alone is all I have needed.

RESOURCES

When the uniform comes off, MVP connects combat veterans and professional athletes so they can create a new, peer-to-peer, support team. Along with weekly workout sessions and Huddles, where members share their struggles and strengths with their brothers and sisters, MVP encourages members to seek additional supportive resources. Below is a list of veteran and athlete organizations MVP members have had the honor of working with.

MVP CONTACT INFO

vetsandplayers.org
info@vetsandplayers.org

LOS ANGELES, CALIFORNIA

losangeles@vetsandplayers.org

LAS VEGAS, NEVADA

lasvegas@vetsandplayers.org

CHICAGO, ILLINOIS

chicago@vetsandplayers.org

ATLANTA, GEORGIA

atlanta@vetsandplayers.org

NEW YORK, NEW YORK

newyork@vetsandplayers.org

SEATTLE, WASHINGTON

seattle@vetsandplayers.org

DALLAS, TEXAS

dallas@vetsandplayers.org

MENTAL HEALTH AND ADDICTION RESOURCES

NATIONAL SUICIDE PREVENTION LIFELINE

Talk: 800-273-8255

Chat: suicidepreventionlifeline.org

The National Suicide Prevention Lifeline is a United States–based suicide prevention network of over 160 crisis centers that provides 24/7 service via a toll-free hotline with the number 1-800-273-8255. It is available to anyone in suicidal crisis or emotional distress.

SAMHSA'S NATIONAL HELPLINE
1-800-662-HELP (4357)

SAMHSA's National Helpline, 1-800-662-HELP (4357), (also known as the Treatment Referral Routing Service) or TTY: 1-800-487-4889 is a confidential, free, 24-hour-a-day, 365-day-a-year, information service, in English and Spanish, for individuals and family members facing mental and/or substance-use disorders. This service provides referrals to local treatment facilities, support groups, and community-based organizations. Callers can also order free publications and other information. Also visit the online treatment locators.

NATIONAL SEXUAL ASSAULT HOTLINE
800-656-HOPE
rainn.org

RAINN (Rape, Abuse & Incest National Network) is the nation's largest anti-sexual violence organization. RAINN created and operates the National Sexual Assault Hotline in partnership with more than 1,000 local sexual assault service providers across the country and operates the DoD safe Helpline for the Department of Defense. RAINN also carries out programs to prevent sexual violence, help survivors, and ensure that perpetrators are brought to justice.

ALCOHOLICS ANONYMOUS (AA)
aa.org

Alcoholics Anonymous is an international fellowship of men and women who have had a drinking problem. It is nonprofessional, self-supporting, multiracial, apolitical, and available almost everywhere. There are no age or education requirements. Membership is open to anyone who wants to do something about his or her drinking problem.

NARCOTICS ANONYMOUS (NA)

na.org

NA is a nonprofit fellowship or society of men and women for whom drugs has become a major problem. They are recovering addicts who meet regularly to help each other stay clean. This is a program of complete abstinence from all drugs. There is only one requirement for membership: the desire to stop using. They suggest that participants keep an open mind and give themselves a break. The program is a set of principles written so simply that anyone can follow them in their daily lives. The most important thing about the principles is that they work.

SMART RECOVERY

smartrecovery.org

Self-Management and Recovery Training (SMART) is a global community of mutual-support groups. At meetings, participants help one another resolve problems with any addiction (to drugs or alcohol or to activities such as gambling or overeating). Participants find and develop the power within themselves to change and lead fulfilling and balanced lives guided by their science-based and sensible 4-Point Program.

THE PHOENIX

thephoenix.org

The Phoenix is a nationwide sober active community for anyone who is in sobriety or a supporter of it. Their mission is to build a sober active community that fuels resilience and harnesses the transformational power of connection so that together all can rise, recover, and live. The only cost of membership is forty-eight hours of sobriety.

VETERANS RESOURCES

VETERANS AFFAIRS

va.gov

Access and manage VA benefits and healthcare.

VETERANS CRISIS LINE

Talk: 1-800-273-8255 Press 1
Text: 838255
Chat: veteranscrisisline.net

Connect with the Veterans Crisis Line to reach caring, qualified responders with the Department of Veterans Affairs. Many of them are veterans themselves.

VET CENTER CALL CENTER

vetcenter.va.gov/index.asp

1-877-WAR-VETS is an around-the-clock confidential call center where combat veterans and their families can call to talk about their military experience or any other issue they are facing in their readjustment to civilian life. The staff is comprised of combat veterans from several eras as well as family members of combat veterans. This benefit is prepaid through the veteran's military service.

NATIONAL CALL CENTER FOR HOMELESS VETERANS

1-877-4AID VET (877-424-3838)

Veterans who are homeless or at risk of homelessness—and their family members, friends, and supporters—can make the call to or chat online with the National Call Center for Homeless Veterans, where trained counselors are ready to talk confidentially 24 hours a day, 7 days a week.

TRAGEDY ASSISTANCE PROGRAM FOR SURVIVORS

taps.org
800-959-TAPS (8277)

TAPS 24/7 National Military Survivor Helpline is always available, toll-free, with loving support and resources at 800-959-TAPS (8277). TAPS provides comfort, care, and resources to all those grieving the death of a military loved one. Since 1994, TAPS has provided comfort and hope, 24/7, through a national peer support network and connection to grief resources, all at no cost to surviving families and loved ones.

ATHLETE RESOURCES

HALL OF FAME BEHAVIORAL HEALTH

hofbh.com
866-901-1241

Hall of Fame Behavioral Health, an affiliate of the Pro Football Hall of Fame, is providing a comprehensive solution for mental health, behavioral health, and substance-use issues for all athletes, their families, and beyond.

NFL LEGENDS COMMUNITY

players.nfl.com

The NFL Player Portal assists football players in navigating the resources and benefits they've earned from the day they're drafted through the rest of their lives. Once players register, they'll have access to the newsletter and all other available benefits.

ABOUT THE AUTHOR

Jay Glazer is a TV personality and National Football League (NFL) insider for FOX Sports' award-winning NFL pregame studio show, *FOX NFL Sunday*, where since 2004, he breaks in with exclusives, late-breaking updates and injury news, and other various reports right up until the start of Sunday's games, and all the way through FOX's Sunday coverage. In 2007, his first year in the studio at FOX Sports, he was named the *Sports Illustrated* Media Person of the Year.

Glazer, his castmates, Terry Bradshaw, Howie Long, Michael Strahan, Jimmy Johnson, and Curt Menefee, and their show, were inducted into the Television Hall of Fame in 2019. He is also part of FOX's *Thursday Night Football.*

Glazer was one of the first ever minute-by-minute breaking online news reporters in the NFL, first for CBSSportsline.com in 1999, followed by FoxSports.com in 2004.

Glazer's many scoops over the years include his obtaining and airing the original New England Patriots' Spygate video (he still has the only copy in existence); breaking the stories of the BALCO drug-lab scandal in the NFL; the end of the NFL lockout; Brett Favre's trade from the Packers to the Jets, as well as Favre's surprise un-retirement and signing with the Minnesota Vikings; Raiders All Pro Barret Robbins going AWOL to Mexico prior to the Super Bowl, and his subsequent suspension from the game; the Giants trading superstar Odell Beckham Jr.; among hundreds and hundreds of others.

Glazer also has been on multiple TV shows, including guest starring on all five seasons of HBO's hit comedy *Ballers* with Dwayne "The Rock" Johnson and John David Washington. In 2015, he hosted the season finale of *Wicked Tuna* for *National Geographic*. He also hosted the one-hundredth episode of *Pitbulls and Parolees* on Animal Planet. He was also a frequent guest star on *The League* on FX.

Football is one of the two sides of Glazer's esteemed sports career; the other being mixed martial arts, where he was the first host of an MMA studio show in America, when he hosted the Pride Fighting Championships in 2004 on *Fox SportsNet*. Glazer hosted MMA shows, such as the UFC and Bellator broadcasts, for fifteen years.

In 2014, Glazer opened the Unbreakable Performance Center in West Hollywood. The gym has become the home to many elite athletes, actors, musicians, and businesspeople. Clientele have included Demi Lovato, Chuck Liddell, Michael Strahan, Wiz Khalifa, Chris Pratt, Sly Stallone, among many others. Unbreakable became one of the first gyms to hire an on-staff mental health therapist in 2021.

Glazer also trains NFL players in mixed martial arts during the off-season. More than one thousand athletes have utilized his training program and have been coached under his Unbreakable system.

In 2015, Jay launched a nonprofit (501c3) charity named MVP (Merging Vets & Players), with former Green Beret Nate Boyer, which works to match up former combat veterans and former professional athletes in order to help one another through the transition into their new lives away from the battlefields and playing fields. MVP opened in seven cities in its first six years, bonding athletes and veterans across the entire country.

In 2021 Glazer was named to the board of the Pro Football Hall of Fame Behavioral Health. He also serves as the spokesman for GNC and has partnered with GNC on a supplements line as well as his MVP charity.

Glazer was raised in Manalapan Township, New Jersey. He attended Pace University, graduating with a degree in mass media in 1993. He then began his writing career as a part-time columnist at the *New York Post* in 1996.